CAST IRON COOKBOOK

Delicious and Easy Cast Iron Skillet Dessert Recipes

(Recipes to Experience the Delicious Difference - Cooking With Cast Iron)

Laurie Goddard

Published by Sharon Lohan

© Laurie Goddard

All Rights Reserved

Cast Iron Cookbook: Delicious and Easy Cast Iron Skillet Dessert Recipes (Recipes to Experience the Delicious Difference - Cooking With Cast Iron)

ISBN 978-1-990334-99-3

All rights reserved. No part of this guide may be reproduced in any form without permission in writing from the publisher except in the case of brief quotations embodied in critical articles or reviews.

Legal & Disclaimer

The information contained in this book is not designed to replace or take the place of any form of medicine or professional medical advice. The information in this book has been provided for educational and entertainment purposes only.

The information contained in this book has been compiled from sources deemed reliable, and it is accurate to the best of the Author's knowledge; however, the Author cannot guarantee its accuracy and validity and cannot be held liable for any errors or omissions. Changes are periodically made to this book. You must consult your doctor or get professional medical advice before using any of the suggested remedies, techniques, or information in this book.

Table of contents

Part 1 1
Introduction 2
Cast Iron Basics..2
Benefits Of A Skillet...4
Cooking In A Cast Iron Pan..5
Recipes 6
Breakfast Recipes...6
    Cheddar Scrambled Eggs..6
    Cheesy Jalapeno Corn Bread..8
    Cast Iron Blueberry Pancakes..9
    Smoked Salmon And Pea Frittata..10
    Cast Iron Popover 12
    Cheesy Potato Hash With Fried Eggs 13
    Onion And Asparagus Omelet..14
    Tex Mex Breakfast Casserole...15
Lunch Recipes..17
    Cast Iron Pizza..17
    Asian Meatballs..18
    Vegetable Samosas With Mint Chutney 19
    Herbed Crusted Chicken...21

- Bacon Creamed Corn 23
- Cheesy Rosti Potatoes 24
- Vegetable Rice Pilaf 25
- Classic Mac'n'cheese 27

Dinner Recipes 28
- Cabbage And Sausage Bake 28
- Italian Style Fish Stew 29
- Chickpea Gnocchi 31
- Rosemary Roasted New Potatoes 32
- Beef Steak With Three-Pepper French Butter 33
- Bacon And Olive Cornbread 35
- Spicy Paella 36
- Mozzarella Turkey Meatballs 38

Desserts Recipes 40
- Plum Upside-Down Cake 40
- Blueberry And Peach Cobbler 42
- Cast Iron Brownies 44
- Spiced Pear Tart Tatin 45
- Skillet Chocolate Cake 46
- Cinnamon Apple Cake 47
- Banana Bread 49
- Giant Chocolate Chip Cookies 51

Conclusion 53

- Part 2 54
- Perfectly Grilled Chicken Breasts 55
- Chili Lime Sweet Potato And Chicken Skillet 56
- Rosemary Skillet Chicken 57
- Homemade Cast Iron Skillet Pizza 59
- Fig And Rosemary Glazed Skillet Chicken 60
- Skillet Honey Lime Chicken 61
- One Skillet Lemon Butter Chicken And Orzo 62
- Skillet Chicken With Brussels Sprouts And Apples 63
- Crispy Chicken Thighs With Smoky Chickpeas 64
- Chicken Mediterranean Recipe With Tomatoes And Green Olives 66
- Crispy Chicken Thighs With Peppers And Salsa Verde 67
- Skillet Mushroom And Spinach Lasagna 69
- Skillet Chicken, Potatoes, And Peppers 70
- Maple-Glazed Skillet Chicken Breasts With Sweet Potato Hash 72
- One Pot Spicy Taco Rice Skillet 73
- Cajun-Style Hash Browns 74
- Ground Turkey Cabbage Skillet 76
- Skillet Meatballs In Marinara Sauce 77
- One Pan Chicken And Spinach Gnocchi 78
- Chicken Enchilada Skillet 79

- Chicken Potpie 80
- Oven-Roasted Kimchi Chicken 81
- Cast-Iron Roast Chicken With Caramelized Leeks 83
- Skillet-Fried Chicken 84
- Roast Chicken With Harissa And Schmaltz 86
- Skillet Chicken Pot Pie With Butternut Squash 87
- . Pan-Roasted Chicken With Harissa Chickpeas 88
- Cast-Iron Roast Chicken With Crispy Potatoes 89
- Perfect Cast-Iron Skillet Chicken Thighs 90
- Mother's Fried Chicken 92
- Southern Fried Chicken With Milk Gravy 93

Vegetables And Sides 94
- Cast Iron Cobbler 94
- Apple Crisp 95
- Black Iron Skillet Corn 95
- Fried Potatoes With Ramps 96
- Southern Greens 97
- Mixed Vegetable Dish 97
- Fried Green Tomatoes 98
- Skillet Fries 98
- Shut Your Mouth Sweet Potato Pie 99
- Sauteed Cherry/Grape Tomatoes 100
- Fat-Free Cinnamon And Sorghum Fried Apples 100

Oven Fried Root Veggies 101

Upside Down Pizza 101

Taco Soup 103

Cheesy Spinach Lasagna 104

Graduated Grilled Cheese 105

Classic Pizza Dough 106

Campfire Pizza 107

Cast-Iron Apple-Blackberry Crumble With Sour Cream Whip 108

Skillet S'mores 110

Skillet Mac And Cheese With Sausage And Bell Peppers . 112

Creole Rice Skillet With Andouille Sausage 112

Skillet Green Beans 113

Potato Cake With Tart Apples And Jarlsberg 114

Savory Dutch Baby 115

Skillet Phyllo Pie With Butternut Squash, Kale, And Goat Cheese 116

One-Skillet Chicken With Buttery Orzo 117

Cast-Iron Pizza With Fennel And Sausage 118

Skillet Peach Cobbler 120

Part 1

Introduction

A cast iron pan, also known as a skillet, may seem like old-fashioned and it may be far from what you would consider a kitchen gadget at a first glance, but the truth behind this is that these types of pans deserve a place in any kitchen out there due to all their advantages and benefits.

Unlike other pans found on the market, cast iron pans conduct the heat perfectly and can go from the stove to the oven and back without having to worry about melting plastic parts or damaging the pan. These cast iron pans are so well made that they will last you a lifetime if maintained properly and generally, the food tastes much better than the one cooked in other kind of pans.

Cast Iron Basics

The first thing to do after buying a skillet is to season it. Seasoning a cast iron pan is what makes it non-stick, it creates a layer that protects the pan and prevents food from sticking to the bottom. Frying eggs, roast chicken or brown potatoes wouldn't be possible without this process.

To season a cast iron pan, wash it well and pat dry it with paper towels or other kind of soft towel, being careful not to scratch the surface at this point. Once the pan is dry, grease it with shortening inside and outside then place the pan in the preheated oven at 400F for 40 minutes. To prevent the fat from dripping and smoking in the oven, place a pan or a tin foil sheet underneath the skillet.

After 40 minutes, turn the heat off and allow the pan to slowly cool down in the oven. Remove the skillet from the oven and wipe off any leftover fat. From now on the pan can be used for any recipe.

If the seasoning is done properly, you won't have to worry about doing it again and all you have to do after using the skillet is to wash it with water and wipe it with paper towels to keep it dry. Try to avoid dish washer soap because it may destroy the non-stick layer you just created through seasoning. Also, avoid washing a cast iron pan in the dishwasher because the hot water and soap will destroy the seasoning. Keep it simple and wash it the old-fashioned way – that's how you maintain a skillet in proper condition!

Compared to the other pans found on the market, there are no chemicals involved in this process and the non-stick layer created is natural and healthy. The so called non-stick pans bought in a store are made by using chemicals which at high temperatures, release into the food. It gets even worse if you scratch the protective layer of the pan. Not only that it releases more chemicals into your food, but it will also make the food stick to the pan and it's impossible to fix, unlike a skillet which can be seasoned again.

A cast iron pan is not only chemical-free, but it is also a versatile addition to your kitchen. You can put skillets on the stove then in the oven and back on the stove again and again and they will remain just as reliable. And they can be used for all sorts of recipes, boosting their taste and crust, their flavor and consistency.

Benefits Of A Skillet

Sturdy – a cast iron pan is heavy and sturdy and it will last you a lifetime if seasoned and maintained properly. Many people have skillets that they've inherited from their grandmothers and they are still in a good condition. And if the pan begins to stick or rust, all you have to do is clean it well and repeat the seasoning process.

Even Cooking – cast iron is a dense metal that heats slowly and holds the temperature for a long time. This makes it great for browning meat and vegetables and for cooking evenly any type of food.

It's Chemical-Free – the seasoning process gives the pan a natural non-stick coating and often this coating gets only better in time as the pan is used more and more.

It Can Be Used On The Stove And In The Oven – having no plastic parts, a skillet can be used both on the stove and in the oven and this makes the pan perfect for foods than need to start on the stove and finish in the oven like steaks or frittatas.

It's Cheap – compared to other non-stick or even ceramic pans found on the market, a cast iron pan is cheap and it comes in various sizes as well. Even better, you can inherit it from a family member and pass it over to your kids later on.

Cooking In A Cast Iron Pan

Cooking in a cast iron pan yields delicious results because the pan and the material that it's made of conduct the heat better and distribute it evenly throughout your food. This makes the pan perfect for frying, searing and baking. And although the pan takes longer to heat up, the cooking is done slower and it allows the flavor to develop properly.

Moreover, the heat is retained long after you remove the pan from the stove so the cooking process continues. This makes the skillet perfect for frittatas, flat bread, roasted chicken, pilaf and a wide range of desserts. In fact, every recipe out there can be adapted for a cast iron pan knowing that the final result will be delicious!

Non-stick pans may not stick, but they are not made for high heat cooking either. Maybe you've noticed, maybe you didn't, but here is a fact: non-stick pans don't brown food well. Food cooked in a non-stick pan simply doesn't have that brown, crisp crust. A cast iron pan, however, can be used over high heat and it browns food beautifully. Moreover, once you brown the food, you can pop it in the oven to finish the cooking process and this would not be possible with other type of pan.

The heavy skillet is perfect for baking because it produces nicely browned, textured baked goods. The heat is so well distributed that the food is cooked all at the same time. Brownies, cakes, cookies and cobblers, but also simple breads, all turn out amazingly into a skillet!

Recipes

The following are some creative recipes you can make using your very own cast iron skillet. I hope you enjoy!

Breakfast Recipes

Cheddar Scrambled Eggs

The rich and flavorful Cheddar is a great match for these scrambled eggs, yielding a creamy and delicious morning meal for the entire family.

Time: 25 minutes

Servings: 4

Ingredients:

2 tablespoons butter

1 shallot, chopped

½ red pepper, chopped

8 eggs, beaten

Salt and pepper to taste

½ cup grated Cheddar

Directions:

1. Heat the butter in a cast iron pan and stir in the shallot.
2. Sauté for 5 minutes until translucent and soft.
3. Mix the red pepper, eggs and Cheddar in a bowl. Adjust the taste with salt and pepper and pour the mixture into your cast iron pan.
4. Cook the eggs until set, stirring often to ensure the creaminess of the dish.
5. Serve the eggs warm with toasted bread.

Nutritional information per serving

Calories: 208

Fat: 15.5g

Protein: 14.8g

Carbohydrates: 2.3g

Cheesy Jalapeno Corn Bread

I love this bread for breakfast because it is filling and I can make it ahead of time. Served with a glass of buttermilk, it's the best way to start your day.

Time: 55 minutes

Servings: 8

Ingredients:

1 ¼ cups cornmeal

1 cup fresh or frozen corn kernels

1 teaspoon baking soda

1 cup buttermilk

1 jalapeno pepper, seeded and chopped

1 cup grated Cheddar cheese

¼ cup melted butter

2 eggs

1 pinch salt

Directions:

1. Combine all the ingredients in a bowl and mix well.
2. Pour the batter into your cast iron pan and place in the preheated oven at 350F for 40-45 minutes or until the edges and top begin to turn golden brown.

3. Remove from the oven when done and let it cool down before slicing and serving.

Nutritional information per serving

Calories: 222

Fat: 12.6g

Protein: 8.1g

Carbohydrates: 20.4g

Cast Iron Blueberry Pancakes

Cast iron pans are great for pancakes because they are non-stick and distribute the heat evenly. With a cast iron pan and this recipe, you are sure to have a delightful breakfast!

Time: 30 minutes

Servings: 6

Ingredients:

1 ½ cups all-purpose flour

2 tablespoons sugar

1 teaspoon baking powder

1 pinch salt

2 eggs

1 ¼ cups whole milk

1 tablespoon lemon zest

2/3 cup fresh or frozen blueberries

2 tablespoons butter or more, as needed

Maple syrup for serving

Directions:

1. In a bowl, combine the flour, sugar, baking powder and salt then stir in the eggs, milk and lemon zest.
2. Mix well then gently fold in the blueberries.
3. Heat the butter in a skillet and drop spoonfuls of batter into the hot pan.
4. Fry on both sides until golden brown and serve the pancakes warm, topped with maple syrup.

Nutritional information per serving

Calories: 225

Fat: 7.3g

Protein: 6.9g

Carbohydrates: 33.2g

Smoked Salmon And Pea Frittata

Having Spanish origins, frittata is a rich and filling dish, but also a versatile recipe. This one asks for smoked salmon and peas, but the possibilities are endless so play with ingredients and come up with a combination that best suits your taste.

Time: 35 minutes

Servings: 6

Ingredients:

6 eggs, beaten

½ cup cream cheese

1 tablespoon chopped dill

1 tablespoon chopped cilantro

1 green onion, sliced

4 oz. smoked salmon, cut into thin strips

1 cup green peas

Salt and pepper to taste

Directions:

1. In a bowl, mix the eggs, cream cheese, dill, cilantro and green onion.
2. Add salt and pepper to taste then fold in the salmon and green peas.
3. Heat a cast iron pan over medium flame then pour the mixture into the pan.
4. Cover with a lid and cook on medium heat for 10 minutes.
5. Place the pan under the broiler for 5-10 additional minutes until the top is golden brown and serve the frittata warm or chilled.

Nutritional information per serving

Calories: 174

Fat: 12g

Protein: 11.9g

Carbohydrates: 4.8g

Cast Iron Popover

Similar to Yorkshire pudding, popovers are great for a quick morning meal. I would pick a random Sunday and spoil my family with this dish next to an omelet or scrambled eggs.

Time: 30 minutes

Servings: 4

Ingredients:

¾ cup all-purpose flour

1 pinch salt

3 eggs

¾ cup milk

4 tablespoons fat (it can be butter, oil or the fat left from a steak)

Directions:

1. Turn your oven on and set it to 400F.
2. Pour the fat in your iron cast pan and place it in the oven.
3. In the meantime, mix the flour, salt, eggs and milk into a bowl.
4. Carefully remove the hot pan from the oven and quickly pour the batter into the hot oil.
5. Cook for 15-20 minutes until well risen and golden brown.
6. Serve the popover warm or chilled.

Nutritional information per serving

Calories: 271

Fat: 17.2g

Protein: 8.1g

Carbohydrates: 20.4g

Cheesy Potato Hash With Fried Eggs

This cheesy dish will surely make your mornings happier!

Time: 40 minutes

Servings: 4

Ingredients:

4 potatoes, peeled and diced

2 tablespoons butter

1 tablespoon vegetable oil

1 shallot, chopped

2 tablespoons chopped parsley

2 garlic cloves, chopped

Salt and pepper to taste

1 cup grated Cheddar

4 eggs

Oil for frying the eggs

Directions:

1. Heat the butter and vegetable oil in a cast iron pan.

2. Stir in the shallot and garlic and sauté for 2 minutes until soft.
3. Add the potatoes and season with salt and pepper.
4. Cook on low to medium flame until the potatoes are tender. Stir often to prevent them from burning.
5. When done, add the parsley and remove from heat.
6. Spoon the hash on serving plates and top with grated cheese.
7. Quickly fry the eggs in vegetable oil and place them over the potato hash.
8. Serve the dish immediately.

Nutritional information per serving

Calories: 345

Fat: 16.3g

Protein: 16.3g

Carbohydrates: 35.4g

Onion And Asparagus Omelet

Gotta love this flavorful, delicious and filling omelet! Asparagus is a great vegetable and easy to cook so this omelet is nothing fancy, yet it tastes great in its simplicity.

Time: 25 minutes

Servings: 4

Ingredients:

1 red onion, sliced

8 asparagus spears, trimmed and sliced

2 tablespoons vegetable oil

1 red bell pepper, cored and sliced

5 eggs, beaten

Salt and pepper to taste

Directions:

1. Heat the oil in a cast iron pan over low to medium flame.
2. Add the onion and sauté until soft and translucent.
3. Throw in the asparagus and bell pepper and cook 5 additional minutes.
4. In a bowl, mix the eggs with salt and pepper to taste and pour this mixture into the pan.
5. Cook on one side until golden brown then carefully flip it over and finish cooking for a few more minutes.
6. Serve the omelet warm.

Nutritional information per serving

Calories: 169

Fat: 12.4g

Protein: 8.5g

Carbohydrates: 6.6g

Tex Mex Breakfast Casserole

This casserole is perfect for a Sunday breakfast or brunch! It may be a slightly spicy dish, but it's not overpowering so kids can eat it too without problems.

Time: 1 hour

Servings: 8

Ingredients:

1 ½ pounds potatoes, peeled and sliced

4 chorizo links, sliced

2 cups enchilada sauce

2 cups grated Cheddar cheese

Salt and pepper to taste

Directions:

1. Layer the potatoes and chorizo in a deep baking pan.
2. Pour the enchilada sauce over the potatoes then season with salt and pepper.
3. Top with grated cheese and cook in the preheated oven at 330F for 50 minutes or until the potatoes are tender and the top is melted and crusty.
4. Serve the casserole warm.

Nutritional information per serving

Calories: 334

Fat: 21.2g

Protein: 16.7g

Carbohydrates: 20.5g

Lunch Recipes

Cast Iron Pizza

Pizza is an all-time family favorite and there is no way that your family says no to a slice of pizza for lunch. This cast iron recipe is easy to make and tastes great. The cast iron acts like a pizza stone, retaining heat, so the cooking process yields an amazing result.

Time: 30 minutes

Servings: 8

Ingredients:

16 oz. pizza dough

½ cup tomato sauce

20 slices salami

2 cups slices mushrooms

2 cups shredded mozzarella

6 basil leaves, shredded

Directions:

1. Place your cast iron in the preheated oven at 400F and let it heat up.
2. Place your dough on a floured working surface and cut it in half.
3. Roll one half of dough in a thin round sheet.

4. Top the dough with tomato sauce, salami, mushrooms and mozzarella, as well as basil leaves.
5. Remove the cast iron from the oven using an oven mitten then carefully transfer the pizza into the skillet.
6. Place back into the oven and cook for 15 minutes or until the edges turn golden brown and crisp.
7. Repeat with the second half of dough and serve the pizzas warm.

Nutritional information per serving

Calories: 456

Fat: 33g

Protein: 19.2g

Carbohydrates: 27.9g

Asian Meatballs

If you're a fan of Asian flavors, these meatballs will be a huge hit! They are tender and flavorful, absolutely delicious served with steamed wild rice.

Time: 50 minutes

Servings: 4

Ingredients:

1 pound ground beef

Salt and pepper to taste

2 green onions, chopped

1 tablespoon brown sugar

2 tablespoons soy sauce

4 garlic cloves, minced

2 tablespoons sesame oil

Directions:

1. In a bowl, combine the ground beef, green onions, brown sugar, soy sauce and garlic.
2. Mix well then adjust the taste with salt and pepper.
3. Heat the oil in a cast iron pan.
4. Form small meatballs and place them into the pan.
5. Fry on all sides until golden brown.
6. Serve the meatballs warm with steamed rice or a salad.

Nutritional information per serving

Calories: 291

Fat: 13.9g

Protein: 35.2g

Carbohydrates: 4.4g

Vegetable Samosas With Mint Chutney

Samosas are an Indian dish usually served on the streets, but you can make your own at home as it's incredibly easy. A cast iron pan is very helpful at cooking them due to spreading the heat evenly.

Time: 1 hour

Servings: 5

Ingredients:

Samosas:

1 ½ cups mashed potatoes

½ cup cooked lentils, drained

1 shallot, chopped

1 tablespoon lemon juice

½ red pepper, chopped

1 pinch cumin powder

1 pinch turmeric

Salt and pepper to taste

10 egg or wonton wrappers

¼ cup vegetable oil for frying

Mint chutney:

½ cup cilantro leaves

2 tablespoons parsley

6 mint leaves

1 shallot, chopped

1 garlic clove

½ green pepper

Salt and pepper to taste

1 lime, juiced

Directions:

1. To make the samosas, in a bowl, combine the mashed potatoes, lentils, shallot, lemon juice, red pepper, cumin powder and turmeric and mix well.
2. Season with salt and pepper.
3. Lay your wrappers flat on your working surface and spoon the filling into each wrapper.
4. Fold the wrappers to form triangles and seal the edges with water.
5. Heat the oil in a cast iron pan.
6. Drop the samosas into the hot oil and fry on both sides until golden brown.
7. Remove the samosas on paper towels.
8. For the chutney, combine all the ingredients in a mortar and mix well with a pestle. Spoon the chutney in a serving bowl.
9. Serve the samosas dipped into the chutney.

Nutritional information per serving

Calories: 361

Fat: 20.9g

Protein: 18.1g

Carbohydrates: 26g

Herbed Crusted Chicken

Stepping out of your comfort zone in terms of food can also mean combining common ingredients into new dishes. The herbed crust is really infusing the mild chicken into a delicious dish.

Time: 50 minutes

Servings: 4

Ingredients:

4 chicken breasts

¼ cup chopped parsley

¼ cup chopped cilantro

2 mint leaves, chopped

Salt and pepper to taste

½ red pepper, chopped

3 tablespoons olive oil

Directions:

1. Place the parsley, cilantro, mint and red pepper in a mortar and mix well until a paste forms.
2. Add salt and pepper to taste.
3. Spread the herb mixture over the chicken.
4. Heat the oil in a cast iron pan.
5. Place the chicken into the oil and cook on both sides until golden brown.
6. Place the cast iron into the preheated oven at 350F for 15 additional minutes.
7. Serve the chicken warm with your favorite side dish.

Nutritional information per serving

Calories: 365

Fat: 21g

Protein: 41g

Carbohydrates: 1.7g

Bacon Creamed Corn

This delicious and rich creamed corn is a great side dish and it's so easy to cook! The flavors are simple, but amazing!

Time: 35 minutes

Servings: 4

Ingredients:

4 ears corn

2 cups milk

1 pinch sugar

1 teaspoon cornstarch

Salt and pepper to taste

4 bacon slices, chopped

Directions:

1. Cut the corn off the ears and place half of it in a blender, together with 1 cup of milk, sugar, cornstarch, salt and pepper.
2. Pulse until smooth.

3. Heat a cast iron pan over medium flame.
4. Stir in the bacon and cook until crisp then stir in the corn and blended corn.
5. Cook on medium flame until creamy and thick, around 15 minutes.
6. Serve the corn warm.

Nutritional information per serving

Calories: 138

Fat: 4.3g

Protein: 6.9g

Carbohydrates: 20.9g

Cheesy Rosti Potatoes

This dish looks like a huge potato pancakes, but it is so delicious! It's a dish that stands out with its simplicity, but the flavors are definitely there and it's incredibly tasty.

Time: 35 minutes

Servings: 4

Ingredients:

4 potatoes, washed and grated

1 green onion, chopped

1 egg

4 bacon slices, chopped

1 cup grated Cheddar

Salt and pepper to taste

Directions:

1. In a bowl, combine the grated potatoes, green onion and egg and stir in salt and pepper to taste.
2. Heat a cast iron pan over medium flame and add the bacon. Cook until crisp.
3. Add the potatoes into the pan and top with cheese.
4. Place in the preheated oven at 350F for 30 minutes or until the top is golden brown and crusty.
5. Serve the rosti warm.

Nutritional information per serving

Calories: 228

Fat: 4.6g

Protein: 12.9g

Carbohydrates: 34.4g

Vegetable Rice Pilaf

Pilaf is a rice dish similar to risotto, but it combines more vegetables and it is made differently, by combining all the ingredients from the beginning of cooking then letting it cook slowly covered with a lid. It's a versatile and delicious recipe if you ask me.

Time: 45 minutes

Servings: 6

Ingredients:

1 shallot, chopped

1 zucchini, diced

1 red bell pepper, cored and sliced

1 yellow bell pepper, cored and sliced

2 ripe tomatoes, diced

1 cup white rice, rinsed

2 tablespoons olive oil

3 cups vegetable stock

1 tablespoon chopped parsley

Salt and pepper to taste

Directions:

1. Heat the oil in a skillet and stir in the shallot. Sauté for 2 minutes then add the vegetables.
2. Cook 5 additional minutes then stir in the rice and cook 5 more minutes, stirring often.
3. Add the stock then season with salt and pepper and cover the cast iron pan with a lid.
4. Cook on low heat for 30 minutes or until most of the liquid has been absorbed.
5. Add the parsley and serve the pilaf warm.

Nutritional information per serving

Calories: 182

Fat: 5.2g

Protein: 3.6g

Carbohydrates: 30.5g

Classic Mac'n'cheese

This classic Mac and Cheese is an easy to make dish and it's a family favorite for many people out there. Cooking it in a cast iron is handy and it makes serving and cleaning later on much easier.

Time: 1 hour

Servings: 6

Ingredients:

12 oz. short pasta

1 ½ cups heavy cream

½ teaspoon garlic powder

4 bacon slices, chopped

2 oz. goat cheese

½ cup grated Parmesan

1 ¼ cups grated Cheddar

½ tablespoon lemon zest

Salt and pepper to taste

Directions:

1. Pour a few cups in a large pot and bring it to a boil with a pinch of salt.

2. Add the pasta and cook until al dente, 8 to 10 minutes. Drain and place aside.
3. Heat a large cast iron pan and add the bacon. Cook until crisp then stir in the heavy cream and bring to the boiling point.
4. Stir in the goat cheese, Parmesan and half of the Cheddar. Mix until melted.
5. Stir in the pasta then top with the remaining cheese and cook in the preheated oven at 350F for 30 minutes or until the top is golden brown and crusty.
6. Serve the mac and cheese warm.

Nutritional information per serving

Calories: 412

Fat: 18g

Protein: 17.3g

Carbohydrates: 44.5g

Dinner Recipes

Cabbage And Sausage Bake

It is a simple dish with common ingredients, but it tastes amazing! In many countries it is a winter dish, but if you choose light sausages, it can be served during summer too.

Time: 1 hour

Servings: 4

Ingredients:

4 chicken sausages

1 head cabbage, shredded

2 tablespoons olive oil

1 shallot, chopped

1 carrot, grated

Salt and pepper to taste

1 cup tomato sauce

½ teaspoon dried thyme

Directions:

1. Heat the oil in a large cast iron pan.
2. Stir in the shallot and carrot and sauté for 5 minutes.
3. Add the cabbage and tomato sauce then season with salt and pepper, followed by the dried thyme.
4. Bring the mixture to a boil and cook 10 minutes then place the sausages on top and place in the preheated oven at 350F and cook for 35 minutes.
5. Serve the dish warm.

Nutritional information per serving

Calories: 203

Fat: 11.7g

Protein: 8.5g

Carbohydrates: 18.3g

Italian Style Fish Stew

This stew combines the tender, delicate fish with tomatoes and beans, plus plenty of Italian herbs to create a delicious and filling dish suited for the entire family.

Time: 1 hour

Servings: 6

Ingredients:

1 tablespoon olive oil

1 teaspoon dried basil

1 red onion, sliced

2 garlic cloves, chopped

1 can diced tomatoes

1 can cannellini beans, drained

4 roasted bell peppers, coarsely chopped

6 halibut fillets

Salt and pepper to taste

Directions:

1. Heat the oil in a skillet and stir in the onion and garlic. Sauté for 2 minutes then add the tomatoes, beans, basil and bell peppers.
2. Season with salt and pepper and bring to a boil. Cook 10 minutes on medium flame.
3. Place the fish fillets over the vegetables and cook in the preheated oven at 350F for 20-25 minutes.
4. Serve the stew warm.

Nutritional information per serving

Calories: 469

Fat: 10.3g

Protein: 58g

Carbohydrates: 23g

Chickpea Gnocchi

The Italians gnocchi are such a simple dish! They can be combined with so many vegetables, but this combination is one of the bests for sure. It's crunchy and flavorful, absolutely delicious.

Time: 35 minutes

Servings: 6

Ingredients:

16 oz. packed gnocchi

2 garlic cloves, chopped

4 bacon slices, chopped

½ teaspoon dried basil

½ teaspoon dried oregano

1 can chickpeas, drained

1 can diced tomatoes

Salt and pepper to taste

Parmesan for serving

Directions:

1. Heat a pot of water over medium flame and bring it to a boil with a pinch of salt.
2. Add the gnocchi and cook as stated on the package. Drain and set aside.
3. Heat a cast iron pan over medium flame and stir in the bacon.
4. Cook until crisp then add the garlic, basil, oregano, chickpeas and tomatoes.
5. Season with salt and pepper and cook for 20 minutes on medium flame.
6. Add the gnocchi and mix gently then serve the dish warm.

Nutritional information per serving

Calories: 249

Fat: 3.6g

Protein: 9.9g

Carbohydrates: 44.5g

Rosemary Roasted New Potatoes

New potatoes are so tender and they make such delicious roasted dishes! But none compares to this recipe. It yields crisp potatoes on the outside and moist and tender on the inside, everything infused with fresh rosemary.

Time: 45 minutes

Servings: 4

Ingredients:

2 pounds new potatoes, washed

4 tablespoons olive oil

1 rosemary sprig

Salt and pepper to taste

Directions:

1. Place the potatoes in a large pot and cover them with water. Cook until inserting a knife into one potato is easy. Drain well.
2. Using the back of a pan, crush each potato slightly then sprinkle them with salt and pepper.
3. Heat the oil in a cast iron pan and add the rosemary.
4. Place the potatoes into the hot oil and cook them on both sides until golden brown.
5. Serve the potatoes warm as a main dish or side dish.

Nutritional information per serving

Calories: 277

Fat: 14.3g

Protein: 3.8g

Carbohydrates: 35.8g

Beef Steak With Three-Pepper French Butter

Beef steak is a classic, but this particular recipe is not. Each of the three peppers has a different aroma and you will love the melting butter infusing the meat on top of the steak. It is a special dish with an amazing flavor, that's for sure.

Time: 30 minutes

Servings: 2

Ingredients:

2 tablespoons butter, softened

1 tablespoon three-peppers mix

½ teaspoon smoked paprika

2 beef steaks

Salt to taste

2 tablespoons vegetable oil

Directions:

1. Place the pepper mix in a mortar and ground it well with a pestle.
2. In a small bowl, mix the softened butter with the peppers and paprika. Add salt to taste then spoon the butter on a plastic wrap.
3. Shape into a log and wrap well then freeze until the steaks are done.
4. Season the steaks with salt then heat the oil in a cast iron pan.
5. Place the steaks into the hot pan and fry on both sides for 4-5 minutes or until the steaks are golden brown.

6. To serve, place the steaks on serving plate and top with a few thin slices of butter.
7. Serve immediately.

Nutritional information per serving

Calories: 390

Fat: 30g

Protein: 26.3g

Carbohydrates: 2.4g

Bacon And Olive Cornbread

This corn bread is great for any time of the day, but I prefer it for a quick lunch or dinner with a glass of buttermilk or replacing the usual bread. It's a savory, flavorful cornbread, absolutely delicious.

Time: 1 hour

Servings: 8

Ingredients:

1 ½ cups all-purpose flour

1 ½ cups yellow cornmeal

2 teaspoons baking powder

½ teaspoon salt

1 2/3 cups whole milk

2 eggs

¼ cup vegetable oil

2 green onions, chopped

4 bacon slices, chopped

½ cup black olives, pitted and sliced

1 pinch black pepper

Directions:

1. In a large bowl, combine the flour, cornmeal, baking powder and salt then stir in the milk, eggs and vegetable oil.
2. Fold in the green onions and black olives and place the bowl aside.
3. Heat a skillet over medium flame and add the bacon.
4. Cook until crisp then pour in the batter.
5. Place the pan in the preheated oven at 350F and cook for 40-45 minutes or until golden brown.
6. When done, remove from the oven and let the cornbread cool down before slicing and serving.

Nutritional information per serving

Calories: 294

Fat: 12.2g

Protein: 7.9g

Carbohydrates: 39g

Spicy Paella

Paella combines various types of seafood into a rich, delicious meat. Despite having such a good taste and exquisite look, paella is simple and you can make it at home with this recipe. A cast iron pan is perfect for it!

Time: 45 minutes

Servings: 8

Ingredients:

1 onion, chopped

3 tablespoons olive oil

4 garlic cloves, chopped

1 green bell pepper, cored and sliced

1 teaspoon paprika

½ teaspoon turmeric powder

1 ½ cups short grain rice

½ cup dry white wine

4 cups vegetable stock

1 pound clams, cleaned

½ pound shrimps, peeled and deveined

4 fish fillets, cubed

Salt and pepper to taste

Lime for serving

Directions:

1. Heat the oil in a large iron cast pan.
2. Add the onion and garlic and sauté for 2 minutes.
3. Stir in the bell pepper, paprika and turmeric then add the rice and cook 2 additional minutes, stirring often.
4. Pour in the wine and cook until evaporated then gradually add the stock and cook until most of the liquid has been absorbed.
5. When the rice is almost done, add the fish, shrimps and clams and cook 10 additional minutes, stirring often.
6. Serve the paella warm, garnished with a few lime slices.

Nutritional information per serving

Calories: 376

Fat: 11.6g

Protein: 16.3g

Carbohydrates: 49g

Mozzarella Turkey Meatballs

The great thing about these meatballs is their hidden mozzarella inside. Cooked in a tomato sauce, they are juicy and loaded with flavor, but when you cut into one, the gooey mozzarella center reveals, boosting their aroma even more.

Time: 1 hour

Servings: 6

Ingredients:

1 ½ pounds ground turkey

2 garlic cloves, chopped

1 potato, finely grated

Salt and pepper to taste

1 teaspoon dried basil

½ teaspoon dried oregano

1 tablespoon chopped cilantro

6oz mozzarella, cut into small pieces

1 can diced tomatoes

½ cup tomato sauce

2 tablespoons olive oil

1 shallot, chopped

1 tablespoon balsamic vinegar

Directions:

1. In a bowl, combine the meat, garlic, potato, basil, oregano and cilantro. Season with salt and pepper and mix well.
2. In a cast iron pan, heat the oil then add the shallot and sauté until translucent.
3. Stir in the tomatoes and tomato sauce and bring to a boil, adding salt and pepper to taste.
4. Mix in the balsamic vinegar and cook for 10 minutes on low heat.

5. In the meantime, form the meatballs. Take small pieces of meat and form small balls, adding a piece of mozzarella in the center of each ball.
6. When the meatballs are done, place them into the boiling sauce and cover with a lid.
7. Cook on low heat for 30 minutes.
8. Serve the meatballs warm with plenty of sauce.

Nutritional information per serving

Calories: 375

Fat: 22.3g

Protein: 40.2g

Carbohydrates: 8.4g

Desserts Recipes

Plum Upside-Down Cake

This juicy, caramelized upside down cake is a delicacy! The moist cinnamon batter is the perfect match for plums, but feel free to replace the fruits with apricots, apples, peaches or even cranberries.

Time: 1 hour

Servings: 8

Ingredients:

¾ cup brown sugar

¼ cup butter, softened

2 eggs

½ cup milk

1 cup all-purpose flour

½ cup whole wheat flour

1 pinch salt

2 teaspoons baking powder

1 teaspoon cinnamon powder

1/3 cup vegetable oil

1 cup white sugar

1 pound plums, halved and pitted

Directions:

1. Heat one cup of white sugar in a cast iron pan and melt it until it has an amber color.
2. Carefully swirl the melted sugar, covering the bottom of the pan and place aside.
3. In a bowl, combine the brown sugar and butter and mix until creamy.
4. Stir in the eggs and milk then add the flours, salt, baking powder and cinnamon and mix well.
5. Add the oil and give it a good mix again.
6. Place the halves of plum on the bottom of your skillet then pour the batter over the plums.

7. Bake in the preheated oven at 350F for 40 minutes or until the top is golden brown.
8. When done, remove from the oven and carefully turn the cake upside-down on a platter.
9. Let the cake cool down before serving.

Nutritional information per serving

Calories: 403

Fat: 16.6g

Protein: 4.6g

Carbohydrates: 61g

Blueberry And Peach Cobbler

This fragrant and juicy cobbler is great for your day to day dessert fix. It's quick to make and incredibly tasty, especially if you top it with a dollop of ice cream.

Time: 50 minutes

Servings: 8

Ingredients:

1 cup fresh or frozen blueberries

6 ripe peaches, sliced

2 tablespoons sugar

1 tablespoon cornstarch

¼ cup butter, softened

¼ cup vegetable oil

½ cup whole wheat flour

2/3 cup all-purpose flour

1 ½ teaspoons baking powder

1 pinch salt

1 cup milk

½ cup brown sugar

½ teaspoon vanilla extract

Directions:

1. In a deep baking pan, combine the blueberries, peaches, sugar and cornstarch. Place aside.
2. In a bowl, mix the butter and oil with the brown sugar until creamy.
3. Stir in the milk and vanilla.
4. Add the flours, baking powder and salt and mix well.
5. Spoon the batter over the fruits and bake in the preheated oven at 350F for 40-45 minutes or until golden brown and crisp on top.
6. Serve the cobbler warm, topped with ice cream, or chilled.

Nutritional information per serving

Calories: 283

Fat: 13.6g

Protein: 3.8g

Carbohydrates: 38.3g

Cast Iron Brownies

These cast iron brownies are dense, moist and absolutely delicious. Plus, they take just a few minutes to make!

Time: 55 minutes

Servings: 8

Ingredients:

½ cup butter, cubed

6 oz. dark chocolate, chopped

1 cup brown sugar

3 eggs

1 cup all-purpose flour

1 pinch salt

Directions:

1. In a heatproof bowl, mix the butter and chocolate and melt them together over a water bath.
2. Stir in the sugar and eggs and mix well.
3. Mix in the flour and salt then pour the batter into a cast iron pan.
4. Bake in the preheated oven at 350F for 30 minutes.
5. Serve the brownies chilled.

Nutritional information per serving

Calories: 365

Fat: 19.6g

Protein: 5.5g

Carbohydrates: 42g

Spiced Pear Tart Tatin

What makes this recipe special is the intense, spices flavor. Cinnamon, nutmeg, cardamom and brown sugar, all come together into a delicious, fragrant dessert.

Time: 45 minutes

Servings: 8

Ingredients:

6 ripe pears, peeled and sliced

½ cup brown sugar

½ teaspoon cinnamon powder

½ teaspoon cardamom powder

1 pinch nutmeg

2 tablespoons butter

1 sheet puff pastry dough

Directions:

1. Spread the butter on the bottom of a cast iron pan.
2. Top with sugar and spices then place the pear slices.
3. Roll the puff pastry into a thin sheet and place it over the fruits.
4. Bake the tart in the preheated oven at 375F for 30 minutes or until well risen and golden brown.

5. To serve, turn the tart upside down on a platter and let it cool down before slicing.

Nutritional information per serving

Calories: 151

Fat: 3.1g

Protein: 0.6g

Carbohydrates: 33.3g

Skillet Chocolate Cake

This skillet cake is so good that it can easily become a celebration cake. It is gooey and moist, absolutely delicious and it tastes even better served with ice cream or a dollop of whipped cream.

Time: 1 hour

Servings: 8

Ingredients:

1 cup all-purpose flour

½ teaspoon baking soda

1 cup white sugar

1 pinch salt

2 tablespoons cocoa powder

¼ cup butter, melted

¼ cup vegetable oil

¾ cup milk

1 teaspoon lemon juice

1 egg

½ teaspoon vanilla extract

Directions:

1. In a bowl, combine the flour, baking soda, sugar, cocoa powder and salt.
2. Stir in the butter, oil, milk, lemon juice, egg and vanilla and mix well.
3. Pour the batter into a skillet and bake in the preheated oven at 350F for 30 minutes.
4. Serve the cake chilled.

Nutritional information per serving

Calories: 285

Fat: 13.9g

Protein: 3.4g

Carbohydrates: 38.9g

Cinnamon Apple Cake

This cake is a classic, but don't underestimate it! It is delicious, moist and fragrant, the perfect cake for your day to day desserts.

Time: 55 minutes

Servings: 8

Ingredients:

Crisp topping:

½ cup all-purpose flour

2 tablespoons sugar

1 pinch salt

½ teaspoon cinnamon powder

¼ cup butter, cubed

1-2 tablespoons cold water

Apple cake:

1 cup all-purpose flour

¾ cup whole wheat flour

1 pinch salt

1 ½ teaspoons baking powder

1/2 teaspoon cinnamon powder

1/3 cup butter, softened

2/3 cup brown sugar

2 eggs

½ cup milk

4 apples, peeled and sliced

Directions:

1. For the cake, mix the flours, salt, baking powder and cinnamon in a bowl.
2. Stir in the butter, sugar, eggs and milk and mix well.
3. Spoon the batter into a skillet and top with apple slices. Place aside.
4. For the topping, combine all the ingredients in a bowl and rub them well until sandy.
5. Spread the topping over the apple slices and bake in the preheated oven at 350F for 40-45 minutes or until the top is crisp and golden brown.
6. Allow the cake to cool down before serving.

Nutritional information per serving

Calories: 375

Fat: 15.2g

Protein: 5.7g

Carbohydrates: 55g

Banana Bread

A cast iron pan is so versatile that you can make pretty much any recipe in it and this banana bread makes no exception. What I love about this recipe is that it uses pieces of bananas into the batter so the final bread is moist and incredibly fragrant.

Time: 1 hour

Servings: 10

Ingredients:

½ cup butter, softened

1 cup white sugar

¼ cup brown sugar

2 eggs

1 teaspoon vanilla extract

2 cups all-purpose flour

2 teaspoons baking powder

1 pinch salt

¼ cup milk

2 bananas, mashed

2 bananas, sliced

¼ cup chocolate chips

Directions:

1. In a bowl, combine the butter and sugars and mix well.
2. Stir in the eggs, vanilla, milk and mashed bananas then add the flour, baking powder and salt.
3. Fold in the banana slices and chocolate chips then pour the batter into a cast iron pan.
4. Bake in the preheated oven at 350F for 40-45 minutes or until fragrant and golden brown.
5. Allow the bread to cool down before slicing and serving.

Nutritional information per serving

Calories: 344

Fat: 11.7g

Protein: 4.6g

Carbohydrates: 55g

Giant Chocolate Chip Cookies

This recipe yields a giant chocolate chip cookie that is crisp, crusty on the outside and moist and gooey on the inside. I have to admit that I love this recipe because it spares me the hassle of baking individual cookies, but it preserves the taste of a traditional cookie.

Time: 55 minutes

Servings: 8

Ingredients:

½ cup butter, softened

¼ cup white sugar

¼ cup brown sugar

2 eggs

½ teaspoon vanilla extract

1 cup all-purpose flour

¼ cup cocoa powder

½ teaspoon baking powder

1 pinch salt

½ cup dark chocolate chips

Directions:

1. Mix the butter and sugars in a bowl until creamy then add the eggs and vanilla.
2. Stir in the flour, cocoa powder, baking powder and salt then fold in the chocolate chips.
3. Spoon the batter into a cast iron pan and bake in the preheated oven at 350F for 30-35 minutes.
4. Let the cookie cool down before slicing and serving.

Nutritional information per serving

Calories: 257

Fat: 15.1g

Protein: 4.1g

Carbohydrates: 29.4g

Conclusion

A cast iron pan may be old-fashioned, but it surely is an asset into your kitchen! Savory or sweet, any recipe tastes better cooked in a skillet and the difference is easy to notice – meat is cooked better, batters rise evenly, steaks are browned perfectly, vegetables are sautéed to perfection as well!

And let's be honest, a cast iron is cheap and reliable – for some reason our grandmothers used this type of pans in the past! And they work great so why not give them a try?

Forget about fancy non-stick or ceramic pans that promise you the moon and the stars. Just go back to the basic and buy the simplest cast iron pan you can find – that's all you'll need in your kitchen to cook great food!

Part 2

Perfectly Grilled Chicken Breasts

Ingredients

- 4 cups water
- ¼ cup sugar
- 2 tablespoons salt
- 2 tablespoons olive oil
- ½ teaspoon black pepper
- 4 chicken breasts
- ½ teaspoon dried garlic
- 2 ice cubed

Instructions:

- Dissolve salt and sugar in the water and soak chicken for 30-60 minutes. (Careful not to soak too long, which can make the meat taste too salty!)
- Preheat a Square Cast Iron Grill Pan on medium-high for 5 minutes. Preheat oven to 350 degrees Fahrenheit.
- Drain chicken, pat dry, and rub with olive oil, garlic, and pepper.
- Sear chicken for 2 minutes on each side. Add ice cubes to the pan and move to the oven. Cook for 18-20 minutes or until the chicken reaches an internal temperature of 165 degrees Fahrenheit.
- Remove from heat and allow to rest 5 minutes before cutting.

Chili Lime Sweet Potato And Chicken Skillet

Ingredients

- 2 tbsp olive oil
- Salt and pepper
- 1 lb chicken breasts, diced into 1" cubes
- 1 green bell pepper, seeds removed and diced
- 1/2 red onion, diced
- 1 tbsp chili powder
- 1/4 tsp cayenne pepper
- 1/2 cup low sodium chicken stock
- 1 can black beans, rinsed and drained
- 1 large (1 lb) sweet potato, diced into 1/2" cubes
- 1 red bell pepper, seeds removed and diced
- 4 garlic cloves, minced
- 1 tbsp cumin
- 1 tbsp paprika
- 1/2 tsp kosher salt
- 2 limes zested
- 1/4 cup cilantro leaves, chopped
- Avocado, sour cream, cheese, etc.

Instructions:

- Heat 1 tbsp olive oil in large skillet. Salt and pepper chicken and then add to pan, cooking for 4 minutes per side or until golden brown. Remove the chicken and set on a plate.
- Add another tbsp olive oil to skillet and reduce heat to medium heat. Add sweet potatoes and cook for 10 minutes, stirring occasionally. Add bell peppers and red onion and

cook for 5 minutes. With 30 seconds left, add garlic and stir in. At this point, the sweet potato should be browning.

- Add in the spices, chicken stock and chicken. Stir so that everything is combined and then cover and cook for about 5 minutes or until sweet potatoes are cooked through.
- Remove from heat and stir in the lime zest and black beans. Adjust for seasoning. Garnish with cilantro, avocado and some lime juice. Serve immediately.

Rosemary Skillet Chicken

Ingredients

- 2-3 pounds of bone-in, skin-on chicken breasts, thighs or drumsticks
- 4 garlic cloves, minced, divided
- 2 tablespoons fresh rosemary, minced
- Sea salt and freshly ground pepper
- 1 tablespoon fresh thyme leaves, minced
- 3½ tablespoons olive oil, divided
- 1 small shallot (about 2 tablespoons), minced
- ¾ cup chicken broth
- 2 tablespoons unsalted butter or ghee, cut into small cubes

Instructions

- First let's get the marinade together for the chicken. In a small bowl, combine together the 2 tablespoons minced rosemary, 2 minced garlic cloves and 2½ tablespoons of olive oil.

- Pat dry chicken and rub the marinade on both sides of the chicken. Cover the chicken, or put it all into a ziploc bag, (that's what I did) and refrigerate the chicken for 1-12 hours. This is a great and easy marinade to make ahead the morning, so when you get home, all you have to do is roast up the chicken.

- When you're home and ready to make dinner, preheat the oven to 400 degrees and place a rack in the lower third of the oven.

- Pat the skin side of chicken dry, and season with salt and pepper.

- Heat remaining 1 tablespoon of olive oil in large ovenproof skillet over medium high heat. I used my 12" cast iron skillet.

- Add chicken, skin side down to preheated skillet, and cook until golden brown, about 5 minutes.

- Flip chicken over and transfer skillet to the oven.

- Roast chicken until an instant-read thermometer inserted in the thickest part of the thigh or breast, registers 165 degrees, about 20-25 minutes. The time varies depending on how large your chicken breasts or thighs are. Chicken breasts take longer to cook than thighs, so note that if you're cooking both together, you will have to remove the thighs earlier in the cooking process.

- Transfer the cooked chicken to a warm plate.

- While the chicken is cooking, prep ingredients for the sauce. Mince the shallot, 2 garlic cloves, thyme leaves, cut up the 2 tablespoons of butter and measure out the chicken broth.
- Take the same skillet that you cooked the chicken in and set it over medium heat. Add to the skillet, the shallot, thyme, and garlic.
- Stir occasionally until the shallot and garlic are softened, about 1½ to 2 minutes.
- Add the chicken broth and cook, scraping up the browned bits, until the broth is reduced by half, about 3 minutes.
- Stir in the 2 tablespoons butter until melted.
- Turn off the heat and pour the sauce into a serving bowl.
- Serve up the chicken and top each piece with the sauce. The sauce is seriously amazing and tastes like gravy. It's the perfect sauce to dip a popover in.

Homemade Cast Iron Skillet Pizza

Ingredients

- 4 oz pizza dough (see notes)
- 3/4 cup mozzarella cheese
- 6 oz pizza sauce
- 2 Tablespoons oil
- 1/4 cup parmesan cheese

TOPPINGS

- 1 Tablespoon fresh basil, chopped
- red pepper flakes

Instructions
- Preheat oven.
- Cut dough ball in half. Form into 10×10-inch circle.
- When pan has preheated; Very carefully use a wad of paper towels/napkins to spread oil in hot skillet. Carefully place dough circle in pan and adjust to fit edges.
- Add sauce —Sprinkle mozzarella & parmesan cheese over top.
- Bake for 14-16 minutes —Repeat cooking process with other dough ball to make second pizza.

Fig And Rosemary Glazed Skillet Chicken

Ingredients:
- 1/4 cup unsalted butter, softened
- 3 sprigs rosemary, destemmed and minced
- 3 cloves garlic, minced
- 1 teaspoon ground black pepper
- 1 fryer chicken, broken into 6 or 8 pieces (I just used 6 drumsticks and 2 thighs both with skins on)
- 2 teaspoons salt

FOR THE SAUCE
- 1/2 cup balsamic glaze
- 1/2 cup fig preserves

Instructions:

- Preheat oven
- Mix butter with half the garlic, half the rosemary, half the salt, and half the pepper.
- Place chicken into skillet then rub the butter on the outside of the chicken pieces.
- Put in the oven to begin roasting.
- Whisk together balsamic glaze, fig preserves, the remainder of the garlic, rosemary, salt, and pepper.
- Pull chicken out, brush sauce and again put it oven. Repeat.
- Cook until chicken has reached an internal temperature of 165 degrees Fahrenheit, about 25 minutes. Pour remainder sauce on top then place skillet aside to cool before serving.

Skillet Honey Lime Chicken

Ingredients

- 1 1/2 pounds boneless skinless chicken thighs chicken breasts will also work
- 2 Tablespoons olive oil
- 1 teaspoon ground cumin
- 1 teaspoon chili powder
- 1/2 teaspoon salt
- 1/4 teaspoon pepper
- 1/2 cup honey
- Juice of one lime
- zest of one lime
- 2 Tablespoons soy sauce

- 1 garlic clove minced

Instructions

- In a medium sized skillet over medium heat add olive oil. In a small bowl combine cumin, chili powder, salt and pepper. Rub on chicken and place in skillet. Cook for 3-4 minutes on each side or until chicken is no longer pink and 165 degrees. Remove chicken and set aside on plate.
- Add honey, lime juice and zest, soy sauce and garlic. Bring to a boil over medium high heat and reduce heat and whisk until it starts to thicken. About 2 minutes.
- Add the chicken back to the skillet and coat in the sauce. Garnish with lime wedges if desired.

One Skillet Lemon Butter Chicken And Orzo

Ingredients

- 2 tablespoons extra virgin olive oil
- 1 pound chicken breasts or small thighs
- kosher salt and pepper
- 1 Meyer or regular lemon, sliced
- 2 tablespoons butter
- 1 clove garlic, minced or grated
- 1 cup orzo pasta
- 1/3 cup white wine
- 2 1/2 cups low sodium chicken broth
- 1/2 a bunch kale, roughly torn
- juice of 1 lemon
- 1 tablespoon chopped fresh dill

Instructions

- 1. Preheat the oven to 400 degrees F.
- 2. Heat the olive oil in a large dutch oven or cast iron skillet set over medium high heat. Season the chicken all over with salt and pepper. When the oil is shimmering, add the chicken and sear on both sides until golden, about 3-5 minutes per side. Remove the chicken from the skillet.
- 3. To the same skillet, add the butter and lemon slices. Sear the lemon until golden on each side, about 1 minute. Remove the lemon from the pan and add to the plate with the chicken.
- 4. To the same skillet, add the garlic and orzo. Cook until the garlic is fragrant and the orzo toasted, about 2-3 minutes. Add the wine to the skillet and de-glaze the pan. Add the chicken broth, kale, and lemon juice. Bring to a boil over high heat and stir. Slide the chicken, lemon slices, and any juices left on the pan back into the skillet. Transfer to the oven and roast, uncovered for 15 minutes or until the chicken is cooked through.
- 4. Serve the chicken topped with fresh dill and lemon zest. EAT!

Skillet Chicken With Brussels Sprouts And Apples

Ingredients

- 1 1/2 lb. boneless, skinless chicken thighs

- 2 tsp. chopped fresh thyme
- Kosher salt and black pepper
- 1 tbsp. canola oil
- 1 (12-oz.) package shredded Brussels sprouts
- 1 sliced apple
- 1/2 sliced red onion
- 1 Chopped Garlic Clove
- 2 tbsp. white balsamic vinegar
- 2 tsp. brown sugar
- 1/3 c. chopped toasted pecans

Instructions:

- Season chicken thighs with fresh thyme, and kosher salt and black pepper. Cook in canola oil in a large skillet over medium-high heat until cooked through, 4 to 5 minutes per side; transfer to a plate.
- Add shredded Brussels sprouts, apple, red onion, and garlic clove to skillet. Cook, tossing, until Brussels sprouts are wilted and onion has softened, 5 to 6 minutes. Stir in white balsamic vinegar and brown sugar. Season with kosher salt and black pepper.
- Return chicken to pan and top with toasted pecans.

Crispy Chicken Thighs With Smoky Chickpeas
Ingredients

- 3 tsp. canola oil
- 8 small bone-in, skin-on chicken thighs
- 1/2 medium onion, chopped
- 3 cloves garlic, chopped
- 1 1/2 tsp. smoked paprika
- 1/2 tsp. ground cumin
- 1 pt. grape tomatoes
- 2 15-ounce cans chickpeas, rinsed
- fresh thyme leaves, For serving
- Kosher salt and freshly ground black pepper
- 1/2 c. plain Greek yogurt

Instructions:

- Preheat oven to 425°F. Heat oil in large ovenproof skillet over medium-high heat. Season chicken with salt and pepper. Cook, in batches, skin side down until skin is browned and crispy, 8 to 10 minutes. Remove chicken to a plate; reserve skillet.
- Add onion and garlic to reserved skillet and cook, stirring occasionally, until starting to soften, 2 to 4 minutes. Stir in paprika and cumin and cook, stirring, until fragrant, 30 seconds. Stir in tomatoes and chickpeas, and bring to a simmer. Season with salt and pepper. Nestle chicken into mixture, skin side up.
- Roast in oven until the internal temperature of chicken reaches 165°F, 20 to 25 minutes.

- Serve sprinkled with fresh thyme leaves and yogurt alongside.

Chicken Mediterranean Recipe With Tomatoes And Green Olives

Ingredients:
- 4 boneless, skinless chicken breasts of equal size
- 2 tbsp minced garlic or garlic paste
- Salt and pepper
- 1 tbsp dried oregano, divided
- Private Reserve extra virgin olive oil
- 1/2 cup dry white wine
- 1 large lemon, juice of
- 1/2 cup chicken broth
- 1 cup finely chopped red onion
- 1 1/2 cup small-diced tomatoes
- 1/4 cup sliced green olives
- Handful of fresh parsley, stems removed, chopped
- Crumbled feta cheese, optional

Instructions

- Pat the chicken breasts dry. On each side of the chicken breasts make three slits through.

- Spread the garlic on both sides; insert some garlic into the slits you made. Season the chicken breasts on both sides with salt, pepper and 1/2 of the dried oregano.

- In a large cast iron skillet, heat 2 tbsp of olive oil on medium-high. Brown the chicken on both sides. Add the white wine and let reduce by 1/2 then add the lemon juice and chicken broth. Sprinkle the remaining oregano on top. Reduce the heat to medium. Cover with a lid or tightly with foil. Cook for 10-15 mins turning the chicken over once (chicken's internal temperature should reach 165 degrees F.)

- Uncover and top with the chopped onions, tomatoes and olives. Cover again and cook for only 3 minutes. Finally add the parsley and feta cheese. Serve with a light pasta, rice or couscous. Enjoy

Crispy Chicken Thighs With Peppers And Salsa Verde

Ingredients

- 1 1/4 c. low-sodium chicken broth
- 1 box roasted garlic-and-olive oil couscous
- 2 tsp. vegetable oil
- 6 large skin-on, bone-in chicken thighs
- 1 1/2 tsp. Kosher salt
- 3/4 tsp. Freshly ground pepper
- 3 medium colorful bell peppers
- 1/2 medium Sweet onion

- 2 clove garlic

Caper Salsa Verde

- 1/4 c. fresh parsley
- 1/4 c. fresh basil
- 1 green onion
- 1/4 c. extra-virgin olive oil
- 2 tbsp. capers
- 1 1/2 tbsp. fresh lemon juice
- salt
- pepper

Instructions:

- Preheat oven to 425 degrees F. Bring broth to a boil in a 12-inch cast-iron skillet. Pour over couscous in a medium bowl; cover and set aside.
- Heat oil in skillet over medium-high heat until very hot. Sprinkle chicken with salt and pepper. Place chicken in skillet, skin sides down, and cook 10 minutes or until skin is browned and crispy. Turn chicken over and cook 4 minutes. Transfer chicken to a plate; discard drippings.
- Sauté peppers and next 2 ingredients 3 minutes. Arrange chicken on top of peppers, skin sides up. Bake at 425 degrees F for 10 minutes or until done.
- Fluff couscous with a fork. Serve chicken and peppers on couscous, and top with desired amount of salsa.

- Stir together parsley, basil, green onion, olive oil, capers, and lemon juice. Season to taste with salt and pepper.

Skillet Mushroom And Spinach Lasagna

Ingredients

- 16 oz. whole milk ricotta
- 1/4 c. chopped fresh basil
- 1 large Egg
- 8 oz. shredded six-cheese Italian blend
- 2 oz. Parmesan
- Kosher salt
- Freshly ground black pepper
- 3 tbsp. olive oil
- 12 oz. assorted mushrooms (such as shiitake, cremini, button)
- 1 medium Sweet onion
- 1 small red bell pepper
- 5 oz. baby spinach or kale
- 2 clove garlic
- 1 can fire-roasted diced tomatoes
- 12 no-boil lasagna noodles
- 10 oz. refrigerated light alfredo sauce

Instructions:

- Preheat oven to 400 degrees F. Stir together ricotta, basil, egg, 1 cup cheese blend, and 1/4 cup Parmesan in a bowl. Season with 1/2 teaspoon each salt and black pepper.
- Heat 1 tablespoon oil in a large skillet over medium-high heat. Add mushrooms and sauté, stirring occasionally, until lightly browned, 5 to 7 minutes; remove to a bowl. Add 1 tablespoon oil to skillet. Add onion and bell pepper and sauté, stirring occasionally, until tender, 4 to 6 minutes. Add spinach and garlic and sauté, stirring, until wilted, 2 to 4 minutes. Add onion mixture and tomatoes to the bowl with mushrooms and stir to combine. Season with salt and pepper.
- Wipe out skillet and coat with remaining tablespoon oil. Arrange 4 noodles in bottom of skillet, breaking as needed to form a single layer. Top with a third each of vegetable mixture, ricotta mixture, and Alfredo sauce. Repeat two more times, layering noodles in opposite direction each time. Top with remaining cup cheese blend and 1/4 cup Parmesan.
- Bake until golden brown, 30 minutes. Serve sprinkled with sliced basil.

Skillet Chicken, Potatoes, And Peppers

Ingredients

- 6 slice bacon
- 1/2 c. canola oil
- 4 small chicken legs

- Kosher salt
- 1 lb. red bliss potatoes
- 2 tbsp. olive oil
- 2 small onions
- 4 small red cherry peppers
- 2 sprig fresh rosemary

Instructions:

- Cut the bacon slices in half crosswise, roll up each piece and secure with a wooden toothpick. Trim the toothpick.
- Heat the canola oil in a large skillet over high heat. Season the chicken with 1/4 teaspoon salt. Add half the chicken to the skillet, skin-side down, scatter the bacon around the chicken and cook until the chicken is golden brown and the bacon is crisp, 4 to 6 minutes per side. Transfer the chicken and bacon to a plate. Repeat with the remaining chicken pieces.
- Wipe out the skillet and return to medium heat. In a medium bowl, toss the potatoes with the olive oil and season with 1/4 teaspoon salt. Transfer the potatoes and any oil in the bowl to the skillet. Arrange the potatoes cut-side down and cook until golden brown and crisp, 6 to 8 minutes. Turn and cook on the rounded sides until crisp, about 2 minutes. Add the onions, peppers, and rosemary and toss to combine. Cook, covered, shaking the pan occasionally, for 5 minutes.

- Return the bacon and chicken (along with any juices) to the pan, nestling it among the vegetables, and cook, covered, shaking the pan occasionally, for 5 minutes.
- Uncover and cook until any liquid has evaporated, the chicken is cooked through, and the potatoes are tender, about 5 minutes.

Maple-Glazed Skillet Chicken Breasts With Sweet Potato Hash

Ingredients

Chicken:

- 1 lb boneless skinless chicken breast cutlets
- Salt and pepper to taste
- 1/2 cup white whole wheat flour
- 2 tablespoons olive oil

Sweet Potatoes:

- 1 tablespoon olive oil
- 2 medium sweet potatoes peeled and diced into 1/2-in cubes
- 1 small onion finely diced
- 2 cloves garlic minced
- 1 teaspoon paprika
- Salt and pepper to taste:

Maple Glaze:

- 1 tablespoon olive oil
- 1 clove garlic minced
- 3 tablespoons balsamic vinegar

- 1/4 cup maple syrup
- Salt and pepper to taste

Instructions

- Pat chicken dry and season with salt and pepper on both sides. Dredge chicken breasts in flour. In a large skillet over medium-high heat, heat oil until shimmery. Place chicken in pan and brown on both sides, 3-4 minutes on each side until golden-brown. Transfer chicken to a plate and set aside for a moment.
- Make the sweet potatoes: heat 1 tablespoon oil in same skillet over medium-high heat until hot. Saute sweet potatoes, onion, and garlic in oil 5-8 minutes until veggies are golden and caramelized (sweet potatoes won't be cooked through) stir in paprika and season with salt and pepper to taste.
- Arrange chicken breasts around the sweet potatoes in skillet. Bake at 400f 20-25 minutes or until chicken registers 165f and sweet potatoes are tender.
- While chicken bakes, make the sauce: in a small skillet over medium-high heat, heat olive oil then saute garlic in oil until just fragrant. Stir in vinegar, syrup, and season with salt and pepper to taste. Bring sauce to a boil, then reduce heat to medium and let simmer until reduced and thickened, about 10 minutes.
- Once chicken is done, drizzle with maple sauce. Enjoy!

One Pot Spicy Taco Rice Skillet

Ingredients

- 1 lb ground beef
- 1 large onion, diced
- 2 bell peppers, diced
- 1 can diced tomatoes with green chilis
- 1 cup salsa
- 1 cup long grain white rice, NOT minute rice
- 1 cup water
- 1 cup beef stock
- 2 tsp cumin
- 1/2 tsp cayenne pepper
- 1 tsp chili powder
- 1 tsp garlic powder
- 1 tsp smoked paprika
- 1 cup shredded cheddar or jack cheese
- green onions, to garnish

Instructions

- In a large pan, brown beef.
- When beef is lightly browned, add diced onions and peppers.
- Cook until beef is fully cooked, onions and peppers are soft.
- Add can of tomatoes with green chili- no need to drain.
- Add salsa, rice, water and stock.
- Stir well to combine.
- Add in spices and mix, cover.
- Let simmer on low until rice is soft and liquid has cooked off.
- Top with cheese, stir in until it melts.
- Serve!

Cajun-Style Hash Browns

Ingredients

- 20 ounces Potatoes O'Brien

- 4 tablespoons butter
- 4 cloves garlic
- 8 ounces Andouille or other smoked sausage, sliced
- 6 eggs (or more if you want, especially if you want to scramble them)
- Cajun seasoning like Tony Chachere's or Tabasco sauce
- 1/2–1 cup shredded pepper jack or sharp cheddar (optional)

Instructions

- Preheat oven to 350. In a 12" (or larger) oven-safe skillet (preferably cast-iron), heat the butter over slightly-hotter-than-medium heat. Melt the butter in the heated skillet and add the garlic and sliced sausage. Cook until the garlic is tender and fragrant. Add the potatoes and cook according to the package/recipe directions until crispy on the outside and tender inside. Season to taste with Cajun seasoning or Tabasco sauce. Remove from heat.

- Using a spoon, make 6 evenly-spaced indentations into the potatoes. Carefully crack an egg into each well and, if desired, sprinkle lightly with Cajun seasoning or salt and Tabasco sauce. Bake in the preheated oven for 18-25 minutes or until the egg whites are completely cooked but the yolks are still runny (mine were done at exactly 20 minutes, but you want a little give or take in each direction). If adding cheese, do it in the last 5 minutes of cooking. Carefully spoon out of the skillet and serve immediately. Makes 6 servings.

Ground Turkey Cabbage Skillet

Ingredients

- 1 medium onion — chopped
- 1 tbsp olive oil
- 1 lb grass-fed extra lean ground turkey
- 2 lbs cabbage — coarsely chopped
- 1 cup homemade tomato sauce — or your favorite tomato sauce
- 1/2 cup vegetable broth
- Salt and pepper
- 1 cup frozen peas
- ½ cup mozzarella cheese — shredded
- Fresh parsley for garnishing

Instructions

- In a cast iron skillet, add olive oil over medium heat.
- Add onion and cook until golden brown, stirring occasionally.
- Add ground turkey and cook for 10 minutes or so, breaking it into small pieces and stirring occasionally.
- Add cabbage and cook for about 5 minutes. Don't forget to stir well.
- Add tomato sauce, broth, salt, and pepper and stir well to combine all the ingredients together.
- Cook for 7 minutes.
- Add peas and cook for more 2 minutes.
- Top with mozzarella cheese and cover the skillet just to melt the cheese. It only takes about 1 or 2 minutes.
- Serve warm topped with fresh parsley.

Skillet Meatballs In Marinara Sauce

Ingredients

- 1 pound lean ground turkey breast
- 1 egg, slightly beaten
- 1/4 cup panko breadcrumbs, gluten-free breadcrumbs if needed
- 1 tablespoon worcestershire
- 1 clove garlic, grated or minced
- 1 teaspoon dried basil
- 3/4 teaspoon dried oregano
- Kosher salt and fresh ground black pepper to taste
- 3 ounces part skim mozzarella cheese, cut into 1/2 inch cubes
- 1/2 cup shredded part skim mozzarella cheese
- 3 cups marinara sauce

Instructions

- In a large bowl combine the ground turkey, egg, panko, worcestershire, garlic, basil, oregano, salt and pepper with your hands.

- Using a small ice cream scoop, scoop the meatball mixture. Take one of the pieces of cubed mozzarella and stuff it into the center of the meatball, making sure to cover the cheese completely with meat. Repeat the process until all of the meat mixture is gone.

- Heat a large skillet over medium high heat and spray it generously with cooking spray or add a tablespoon of olive oil. Place the meatballs in the skillet and brown them for 2 minutes on each side.

- Pour the marinara sauce evenly into the skillet and turn the heat down to medium low. Cover the skillet with a lid and simmer the meatballs for 10 minutes. Top the meatballs with the shredded mozzarella and serve.

One Pan Chicken And Spinach Gnocchi

Ingredients

- 1 tablespoon olive oil
- 2 cups sliced mushrooms
- 1 small yellow onion chopped
- 1 and 1/2 teaspoons minced garlic
- 4 tablespoons butter
- 1/4 cup white flour
- 2 teaspoons chicken seasoning
- Salt and pepper
- 1/4 teaspoon ground cayenne pepper optional
- 2 cups milk (2% or whole. 1% works as a lighter but less creamy meal)
- 1 and 1/4 cups chicken broth
- 1 package (16 ounces) gnocchi
- 2 cups prepared rotisserie chicken
- 2 cups spinach
- 1/2 cup parmesan cheese
- Optional: fresh parsley, salt and pepper

Instructions

- Move a rack in your oven to the upper third of the oven and then preheat to 425 degrees F.
- Place a large oven-safe skillet (I use a 12 inch lodge skillet) on the stove over medium-high heat. Pour in the olive oil.

- Add in the mushrooms and chopped onion and stir until the onion is transparent and mushrooms lightly browned or about 5-6 minutes. Add in the garlic and stir for another 30 seconds. Remove to a small bowl or plate and quickly wipe out the skillet.
- Place the butter in the skillet and melt. Gradually whisk in the flour until smooth, and continue cooking, whisking constantly for about 3 minutes. Add in the chicken seasoning, about 1/2 teaspoon salt, 1/4 teaspoon pepper, and cayenne pepper if desired.
- Very gradually whisk in the milk and chicken broth until the mixture is smooth. While whisking constantly allow the mixture to thicken (about 5 minutes).
- Add in the prepared chicken (remove skin and bones and shred or cut into small pieces OR use prepared rotisserie chicken that has already been cut into pieces), gnocchi (uncooked), cooked mushrooms and onions mixture, and spinach. Stir until all is coated.
- Top with Parmesan cheese and place in the oven.
- Bake for 17-22 minutes. If desired, turn on the broiler and then broil for another 2-3 minutes for a delicious crispy top.
- Remove from the heat, top with additional salt, pepper, and some chopped fresh parsley if desired. Enjoy immediately.

Chicken Enchilada Skillet

Ingredients
- 12 corn tortillas cut into bite sized pieces
- 3 cups shredded or chopped cooked chicken
- 10 ounces Ro*Tel Diced Tomatoes and Green Chiles 1 can

- 10 ounces red enchilada sauce 1 can
- 8 ounces tomato sauce 1 can
- 1/2 cup grated Cheddar
- 1/2 cup grated Monterey Jack
- 1/2 avocado sliced thin
- 1/4 cup chopped cilantro

Instructions

- Spray a large skillet with non-stick cooking spray and heat the pan over medium heat.
- Add the corn tortillas and cooked chicken to the pan and cook until heated through, stirring often.
- Pour the undrained Ro*Tel, enchilada sauce, and tomato sauce into the pan with 1/4 cup of each cheese. Stir to combine well. Cover and cook 5 minutes or until hot and bubbly.
- Sprinkle on the remaining cheese, top with the avocado and cilantro before serving.

Chicken Potpie

Ingredients

- 2 tbsp. unsalted butter
- 1 medium onion
- 4 medium carrots
- 2 stalk celery
- 2 clove garlic
- 1/2 tsp. salt

- 1/2 tsp. Freshly ground pepper
- 2 tbsp. all-purpose flour
- 3 tbsp. heavy cream
- 2 c. chicken broth
- 4 c. shredded cooked chicken
- 1 c. frozen peas
- 1 1/2 tbsp. chopped fresh dill
- 1 store-bought piecrust
- 1 Egg

Instructions:

- Preheat oven to 400 degrees F. Heat butter in a 12-inch cast-iron skillet over medium heat. Add onion, carrots, celery, and garlic and cook until carrots begin to soften, about 6 minutes. Season with salt and pepper.
- Reduce heat to medium-low and stir in flour. Cook for 1 minute. Stir in heavy cream and broth, using a whisk, until combined. Stir in chicken, peas, and dill and bring to a boil. Remove from heat.
- Gently roll out store-bought pie crust until it reaches 12 inches in diameter. Place dough atop chicken mixture and brush with egg; cut vents in pastry. Transfer skillet to oven; bake until crust is browned and flaky, about 35 minutes.

Oven-Roasted Kimchi Chicken

Ingredients

- 6 tablespoons unsalted butter, room temperature
- Kimchi Butter
- ⅓ cup kimchi plus 1 tablespoon kimchi juice
- ¼ teaspoon kosher salt

Chicken

- 2 tablespoons coriander seeds
- 1 teaspoon crushed red pepper flakes
- 1 teaspoon finely grated lemon zest
- ½ teaspoon black peppercorns
- ¼ teaspoon cumin seeds
- 4 teaspoons kosher salt, plus more
- 1 3½–4-pound chicken, backbone removed
- 1 pound fingerling potatoes
- 4 ounces thick-cut bacon, cut into 1-inch pieces
- 2 ears of corn, husked, cut crosswise into 3-inch pieces

Special Equipment

- A spice mill or a mortar and pestle

Instructions:

Kimchi Butter

- Pulse butter, kimchi and kimchi juice, and salt in a food processor, scraping down sides as needed, until kimchi is finely chopped and fully incorporated into butter. Cover and store at room temperature.
- **Do Ahead:** Kimchi butter can be made 3 days ahead. Chill.

Chicken

- Grind coriander seeds, red pepper flakes, lemon zest, black peppercorns, cumin seeds, and 4 tsp. salt in a spice mill or with a mortar and pestle until very finely ground.

- Place chicken, skin side up, on a rimmed baking sheet. Using the heel of your hands, press firmly on breastbone to flatten. Season chicken on both sides with ¼ cup spice mixture, patting to adhere. Chill, uncovered, 3–8 hours.
- Boil potatoes in salted water until just tender, 15–20 minutes. Remove from heat and let sit uncovered until ready to use (up to 5 hours).
- Preheat oven to 550° (or maximum setting). Place chicken on a foil-lined rimmed baking sheet, leaving wings untucked. Place half of the kimchi butter in small pieces over the chicken and roast until browned but not fully cooked, 20–25 minutes. Arrange bacon, potatoes, and corn around chicken; sprinkle with reserved spice mixture. Roast until an instant-read thermometer inserted into the thickest part of the thigh registers 165°, 10–15 minutes. Transfer to a cutting board and let chicken rest 10 minutes before carving.
- Transfer bacon and vegetables to a large bowl and add remaining kimchi butter; toss to melt butter and coat vegetables. Serve alongside chicken.

Cast-Iron Roast Chicken With Caramelized Leeks

Ingredients

- 1 3½–4-pound whole chicken
- Kosher salt
- 3 leeks, white and pale green parts only, halved lengthwise
- 3 tablespoons olive oil, divided
- Freshly ground black pepper

Instructions:

- Pat chicken dry with paper towels and season generously with salt, inside and out. (We use 1 tsp. Diamond Crystal or ½ tsp. Morton kosher salt per lb.) Tie legs together with kitchen twine. Let sit 1 hour to allow salt to penetrate, or chill, uncovered, up to 1 day ahead.
- Place a rack in upper third of oven and set a 12" cast-iron skillet or 3-qt. enameled cast-iron baking dish on rack. Preheat oven to 425°.
- Meanwhile, toss leeks and 2 Tbsp. oil in a medium bowl to coat; season with salt and pepper.
- Once oven reaches temperature, pat chicken dry with paper towels and lightly coat with half of the remaining oil; sprinkle with dry rub, if using. Drizzle remaining oil into hot skillet (this helps keep the chicken from sticking and tearing the skin). Place chicken in the center of skillet and arrange leeks around. Roast until leeks are browned at edges and tender and an instant-read thermometer inserted into the thickest part of breasts registers 155°, 50–60 minutes (temperature will climb to 165° as chicken rests). Let chicken rest in skillet at least 20 minutes and up to 45 minutes.
- Transfer chicken to a cutting board and carve. Serve with leeks.

Skillet-Fried Chicken

Ingredients
- 2 tablespoons kosher salt, divided
- 2 teaspoons plus 1 tablespoon freshly ground black pepper
- 1 1/2 teaspoons paprika
- 3/4 teaspoon cayenne pepper
- 1/2 teaspoon garlic powder
- 1/2 teaspoon onion powder

- 1 3–4-lb. chicken (not kosher), cut into 10 pieces, backbone and wing tips removed
- 1 cup buttermilk
- 1 large egg
- 3 cups all-purpose flour
- 1 tablespoon cornstarch
- Peanut oil (for frying)

Instructions

- Whisk 1 Tbsp. salt, 2 tsp. black pepper, paprika, cayenne, garlic powder, and onion powder in a small bowl. Season chicken with spices. Place chicken in a medium bowl, cover, and chill overnight.
- Let chicken stand covered at room temperature for 1 hour. Whisk buttermilk, egg, and 1/2 cup water in a medium bowl. Whisk flour, cornstarch, remaining 1 Tbsp. salt, and remaining 1 Tbsp. pepper in a 9x13x2" baking dish.
- Pour oil into a 10"–12" cast-iron skillet or other heavy straight-sided skillet (not nonstick) to a depth of 3/4". Prop deep-fry thermometer in oil so bulb is submerged. Heat over medium-high heat until thermometer registers 350°. Meanwhile, set a wire rack inside a large rimmed baking sheet.
- Working with 1 piece at a time (use 1 hand for wet ingredients and the other for dry ingredients), dip chicken in buttermilk mixture, allowing excess to drip back into bowl. Dredge in flour mixture; tap against bowl to shake off excess. Place 5 pieces of chicken in skillet. Fry chicken, turning with tongs every 1–2 minutes and adjusting heat to maintain a steady temperature of 300°–325°, until skin is deep golden brown and an instant-read thermometer inserted into thickest part of chicken registers 165°, about 10 minutes for wings and 12 minutes for thighs, legs, and breasts.

- Using tongs, remove chicken from skillet, allowing excess oil to drip back into skillet; transfer chicken to prepared rack.

Roast Chicken With Harissa And Schmaltz

Ingredients

- 3 garlic cloves, smashed, peeled
- ⅓ cup sugar
- ¼ cup coriander seeds
- 1 cup kosher salt, plus more
- 1 4–4½-pound chicken, halved, backbone removed
- 1 cup Three-Chile Harissa
- ¼ cup schmaltz (chicken fat) or olive oil

Instructions

- Bring garlic, sugar, coriander seeds, 1 cup kosher salt, and 8 cups water to a boil in a large saucepan, stirring to dissolve sugar and salt. Transfer to a large bowl and add 1 cup ice. Let cool. (You can also refrigerate or freeze brine if you want to speed things up.)
- While brine is cooling, bone chicken breasts, leaving leg and thigh quarters intact. Start by cutting off wing tips; discard. Place chicken, skin side down, on a cutting board. Working with 1 chicken half at a time, angle the blade of a thin, sharp knife flush against breast bone and cut along bone to separate the rib cage from flesh. The only bones remaining should be in the wing, thigh, and drumstick. Repeat on the other side (save bones for making your next pot of stock).
- Place chicken halves in cooled brine. Cover tightly and chill 12 hours.
- Transfer chicken to a rimmed baking sheet or baking pan and pick off coriander seeds. Spread harissa all over chicken. Cover tightly and chill at least 1 hour and up to 12 hours.

- Preheat oven to 400° (if you have a convection oven, turn the convection fan on). Heat schmaltz in a large cast-iron pan over medium. Carefully place chicken halves, skin sides down, in pan, making sure all the skin is in the fat. Cook until skin darkens and starts to crisp, about 5 minutes. Transfer skillet to oven and roast chicken until skin is very dark and meat is more than halfway cooked through, 20–25 minutes.
- Remove skillet from oven and carefully turn chicken. Return to oven and roast, skin side up, until an instant-read thermometer inserted into the thickest part of thigh registers 165°, 8–12 minutes.
- Transfer chicken to a large platter, placing skin side up. Drizzle some of the schmaltz over chicken and serve remaining schmaltz alongside.

Skillet Chicken Pot Pie With Butternut Squash

Ingredients
- ¼ cup olive oil
- 1 cup frozen white pearl onions, thawed
- 4 garlic cloves, finely chopped
- 1 tablespoon chopped fresh sage
- 1 small bunch kale, center ribs and stems removed, leaves chopped
- Kosher salt, freshly ground pepper
- ¼ cup all-purpose flour
- 3 cups low-sodium chicken broth
- ½ small butternut squash, peeled, cut into ½-inch pieces (about 1½ cups)
- ½ rotisserie chicken, meat torn into bite-size pieces (about 1½ cups)

- 1 sheet frozen puff pastry (such as Dufour or Pepperidge Farm), thawed
- 1 large egg

Instructions:

- Place a rack in upper third of oven; preheat to 425°. Heat oil in an 8-inch cast-iron or other heavy ovenproof skillet over medium-high heat. Add onions; cook, stirring occasionally, until beginning to brown, about 4 minutes.
- Reduce heat to medium-low. Add garlic and sage to skillet and cook, stirring occasionally, until garlic begins to brown, about 2 minutes.
- Add kale and season with salt and pepper. Cook, tossing often, until wilted, about 4 minutes. Sprinkle flour over. Cook, stirring constantly, about 4 minutes.
- Stir in broth, ½-cupful at a time, then add squash. Bring to a boil, reduce heat, and simmer until squash is just softened and broth is thickened, 8-10 minutes. Add chicken to skillet, stir, and season with salt and pepper.
- Unfold pastry and smooth any creases; place over skillet, allowing corners to hang over sides. Whisk egg and 1 teaspoon water in a small bowl. Brush pastry with egg wash; cut four 1-inch slits in top to vent.
- Bake pot pie until pastry is beginning to brown, 15-20 minutes. Reduce oven temperature to 375° and bake until pastry is deep golden brown and crisp, 15-20 minutes longer. Let cool for 10 minutes before serving.

. Pan-Roasted Chicken With Harissa Chickpeas

Ingredients

- 1 tablespoon olive oil
- 8 skin-on, bone-in chicken thighs (about 3 lb.)

- Kosher salt and freshly ground black pepper
- 1 small onion, finely chopped
- 2 cloves garlic, finely chopped
- 2 tablespoons tomato paste
- 2 15-oz. cans chickpeas, rinsed
- ¼ cup harissa paste
- ½ cup low-sodium chicken broth
- ¼ cup chopped fresh flat-leaf parsley
- Lemon wedges, for serving
- Harissa, a spicy North African red chile paste, is available at Middle Eastern markets, some specialty foods stores, and online.

Instructions:

- Preheat oven to 425°. Heat oil in a large ovenproof skillet over medium-high heat. Season chicken with salt and pepper. Working in 2 batches, cook until browned, about 5 minutes per side; transfer to a plate.
- Pour off all but 1 Tbsp. drippings from pan. Add onion and garlic; cook, stirring often, until softened, about 3 minutes. Add tomato paste and cook, stirring, until beginning to darken, about 1 minute. Add chickpeas, harissa, and broth; bring to a simmer.
- Nestle chicken, skin side up, in chickpeas; transfer skillet to oven. Roast until chicken is cooked through, 20–25 minutes. Top with parsley and serve with lemon wedges for squeezing over.

Cast-Iron Roast Chicken With Crispy Potatoes

Ingredients

- 1 3½–4-pound whole chicken

- Kosher salt
- 1½ pounds russet potatoes, scrubbed, thinly sliced crosswise
- 2 tablespoons unsalted butter, melted
- 1 tablespoon thyme leaves
- 2 tablespoons olive oil, divided
- Freshly ground black pepper

Instructions:

- Pat chicken dry with paper towels and season generously with salt, inside and out. (We use 1 tsp. Diamond Crystal or ½ tsp. Morton kosher salt per lb.) Tie legs together with kitchen twine. Let sit 1 hour to allow salt to penetrate, or chill, uncovered, up to 1 day ahead.
- Place a rack in upper third of oven and set a 12" cast-iron skillet or 3-qt. enameled cast-iron baking dish on rack. Preheat oven to 425°.
- Meanwhile, toss potatoes, butter, thyme, and 1 Tbsp. oil in a large bowl to coat; season with salt and pepper.
- Once oven reaches temperature, pat chicken dry with paper towels and lightly coat with half of remaining oil; sprinkle with dry rub, if using. Drizzle remaining oil into hot skillet (this helps keep the chicken from sticking and tearing the skin). Place chicken in the center of skillet and arrange potatoes around. Roast until potatoes are golden brown and crisp and an instant-read thermometer inserted into the thickest part of breasts registers 155°, 50–60 minutes (temperature will climb to 165° as chicken rests). Let chicken rest in skillet at least 20 minutes and up to 45 minutes.
- Transfer chicken to a cutting board and carve. Serve with potatoes.

Perfect Cast-Iron Skillet Chicken Thighs

Ingredients

- 6 skin-on, bone-in chicken thighs (about 2 1/4 pounds)
- Kosher salt and freshly ground pepper
- 1 tablespoon vegetable oil

Recipe preparation

- Preheat oven to 475°. Season chicken with salt and pepper. Heat oil in a 12" cast-iron or heavy nonstick skillet over high heat until hot but not smoking. Nestle chicken in skillet, skin side down, and cook 2 minutes. Reduce heat to medium-high; continue cooking skin side down, occasionally rearranging chicken thighs and rotating pan to evenly distribute heat, until fat renders and skin is golden brown, about 12 minutes.
- Transfer skillet to oven and cook 13 more minutes. Flip chicken; continue cooking until skin crisps and meat is cooked through, about 5 minutes longer. Transfer to a plate; let rest 5 minutes before serving.

PAN-SEARED SAUSAGE WITH LADY APPLES AND WATERCRESS

Ingredients

- 1 tablespoon olive oil
- 1 pound lady apples, halved through stem ends
- 1½ pound sweet Italian sausages
- ¼ cup dry white wine
- 2 tablespoons white wine vinegar
- 1 bunch watercress, trimmed (about 6 cups)
- Kosher salt and freshly ground black pepper

Instructions:

- Heat oil in a large cast-iron or other heavy skillet over medium-high heat. Add apples, cut side down, and cook, turning occasionally, until golden brown, 5–8 minutes.
- Prick sausages with a fork, add to skillet with apples, and cook, turning occasionally, until browned, 10–12 minutes. Add wine and vinegar to skillet. Bring to a boil, reduce heat, and simmer until thickened (liquid should coat a spoon), about 4 minutes. Add watercress and toss to coat; season with salt and pepper.
- Serve with pan juices spooned over.

Mother's Fried Chicken

Ingredients:

- ½ teaspoon salt
- 1 teaspoon sugar
- ¼ teaspoon pepper
- ¼ cup Canola oil
- 6 chicken legs
- ½ cup flour
- 1 egg
- Garlic salt, optional

Instructions:

- Mix salt, pepper, sugar and flour.
- Put oil in cast iron; heat on low.
- Roll chicken in egg, then flour mixture.
- Fry chicken.

Southern Fried Chicken With Milk Gravy

Ingredients:

- 2 eggs
- 1¼ cup all-purpose flour
- 2 tablespoons milk
- ¼ teaspoon ground cumin
- ¼ teaspoon paprika
- 1 cup shortening
- 2 broiler/fryer-type chickens, cut up (3½ pounds each)
- 1½ teaspoons pepper
- ¼ teaspoon dried oregano

Milk Gravy:

- 3 cup all-purpose flour
- 2 teaspoon salt
- half teaspoon pepper
- 1 cup milk
- 1 cup water
- half teaspoon browning sauce, optional
- Fresh oregano, optional

Instructions:

- Mix eggs and milk.

- Combine flour and seasonings.
- Dip chicken pieces in egg mixture, then flour mixture.
- Melt shortening in skillet; brown chicken on both sides.
- Cover and cook over low heat.

- **Milk Gravy:** stir flour, salt and pepper.
- Cook and stir until browned.
- Combine milk and water; add to fryer, stirring constantly until it thickens.
- Add browning sauce if desired.

Vegetables And Sides

Cast Iron Cobbler

Ingredients:

- 2 20-ounce cans pie filling (your choice)
- 3 tablespoons butter
- 1 white or yellow cake mix
- 1 cup 7-Up® Ice cream or whipped topping, optional

Instructions:

- Pour pie filling in a skillet and sprinkle cake mix over the pie. Slice butter over the top. Pour the 7-Up® over everything. Bake.

Apple Crisp

Ingredients:

- 1½ cups quick oats
- 1 teaspoon cinnamon
- 1 cup brown sugar
- 1 stick butter
- ½ cup flour
- 1 can apple pie filling

Instructions:

- Mix oats, brown sugar, cinnamon and flour in butter.
- Put apple filling in the bottom of skillet. Sprinkle crumbled mixture on top of filling.
- Bake.

Black Iron Skillet Corn

Ingredients:

- 4 tablespoons flour
- Salt and pepper to taste
- 6 slices bacon
- ½ pound bacon

- 1 cup milk
- 8 ears of corn, fresh
- ½ cup water

Instructions:

- Fry bacon in cast iron.
- Add corn to bacon drippings.
- Cook on low heat, stirring constantly. Then add a little water and cook until water is gone.
- Mix flour into milk. Add corn, crumbled bacon, salt and pepper.
- Cook a few minutes longer to thicken the white sauce.

Fried Potatoes With Ramps

Ingredients:

- 6 potatoes, sliced ½" thick
- 1 tablespoon sugar
- 1 cup ramps, chopped (use entire plant if good)
- Salt and pepper, to taste
- Bacon drippings

Instructions:

- In large cast iron skillet, add bacon drippings; combine potatoes, ramps, and sugar.
- Cook over medium to low heat until potatoes are tender.

- Season with salt and pepper.

Southern Greens

Ingredients:

- ½ cup Appalachian Mountain
- Salad Dressing
- Specialty Wilted Lettuce
- 2 pounds fresh assorted greens (Kale, Collard, Mustard and Turnip)

Instructions:

- In iron pan, heat salad dressing.
- Add fresh greens; sauté.
- Simmer in dressing about 30 minutes.

Mixed Vegetable Dish

Ingredients:

- 1 green pepper
- Salt and pepper to taste
- 1 6-ounce jar or can mushrooms, sliced (or fresh)
- 1 tablespoon butter
- 2 turnips
- 2 tablespoons olive oil
- 3 potatoes
- 2 onions

Instructions:

- In iron skillet, heat olive oil and butter.
- Slice and dice vegetables; cook in skillet.

Fried Green Tomatoes

Ingredients:

- 3 tablespoons canola oil
- ½ cup flour
- 2-3 large green tomatoes, sliced
- ¼ teaspoon pepper
- Fried potatoes, optional
- ½ teaspoon salt
- Biscuits, optional

Instructions:

- In iron skillet, heat oil on low.
- Roll sliced tomatoes in flour; place in pan.
- Add salt and pepper and cook on low.

Skillet Fries

Ingredients:

- 4 cups potatoes, raw, thinly sliced (about 2 pounds)
- 1 teaspoon salt
- 2 medium onions, thinly sliced
- ¼ cup bacon fat or lard

- ½ teaspoon pepper

Instructions:

- Toss potatoes, onions and seasonings together.
- Heat bacon fat in a pan; add potato mixture. Cover and cook.

Shut Your Mouth Sweet Potato Pie

Ingredients:

Pie Filling:

- 3 pounds yams
- 1½ cups sugar
- 1 stick of butter
- 2 eggs
- 1½ teaspoon nutmeg
- 1 can evaporated milk
- 1 teaspoon vanilla extract
- Dash of cinnamon

Pie Crust:

- 2 cups of flour
- ½ teaspoon salt
- a cup plus 1 tablespoon of shortening
- 3 tablespoons ice water

Instructions:

- Bake yam.

Sauteed Cherry/Grape Tomatoes

Ingredients:

- 1 tablespoon olive oil
- 6 green onions, thinly sliced with some stems
- 3 garlic cloves, finely chopped
- ¼ cup Appalachian Mountain
- Salad Dressing®
- 1 pint fresh cherry/grape tomatoes
- Specialty Wilted Lettuce
- Salt to taste.

Instructions:

- Preheat oven.
- Sauté onions and garlic in oil. Add tomatoes, dressing and salt, place in oven; roast 18-20 minutes.

Fat-Free Cinnamon And Sorghum Fried Apples

Ingredients:

- 4 cups apples, tart, firm, pieced or sliced, cores removed
- ¼ teaspoon cinnamon
- ¼ cup sorghum molasses
- ¼ cup water

Instructions:

- Place apple pieces in a cast iron skillet.
- Add water and sorghum.
- Add cinnamon.
- Cook until water is gone and apples begin to caramelize in the molasses.

Oven Fried Root Veggies

Ingredients:

- ½ teaspoon salt
- 1 teaspoon rosemary, dried
- ¼ teaspoon black pepper
- 6 cups assorted root vegetables, chopped 1" thick
- ½ teaspoon red pepper flakes
- 2 tablespoons Brown's Creations' Garlic Infused Oil®

Instructions:

- In iron skillet, toss vegetables until cooked.
- Add salt, black pepper, dried rosemary and red pepper flakes to taste.
- Bake.

Upside Down Pizza

Ingredients:

Filling:
- ½ pound sweet (or hot) sausage
- 1 medium onion, chopped
- 1 pound hamburger
- ¾ teaspoon Italian seasonings
- 1½ 14-ounce jars pizza sauce
- 2 tablespoons cooking oil
- ¾ teaspoon garlic powder
- 2 cups Mozzarella cheese, grated

Dough:
- 2 eggs
- ¼ teaspoon salt
- 1 cup milk
- 1½ cups flour

Topping:
- ½ cup Parmesan cheese, grated

Instructions:
- Add oil to iron skillet.
- Add sausage, hamburger and onion.
- Add garlic powder, Italian seasonings and pizza sauce.
- Add grated Mozzarella cheese on top of mixture.
- Combine and mix eggs, milk, salt and flour. Spread over meat mixture.

- Sprinkle with grated cheese.
- Bake.

Taco Soup

Ingredients:

- 2 pounds lean ground beef
- Shredded Cheddar Cheese for garnish
- 1 can (15 oz) white whole kernel corn with liquid
- 1 can (15 oz) black beans with liquid
- 1 can (28 oz) diced tomatoes with green chilies
- 2 large onions, chopped
- 2 cans (14 oz) chicken broth
- 2 cans (15 oz) Mexican-style chili beans with liquid
- 2 cans (10 oz) Rotel tomatoes with green chilies
- 2 large onions, chopped 2 cans (15 oz)
- 1 package Ranch dressing mix
- 1 can (15 oz) tomato sauce
- Tortilla chips for garnish
- 2 cans (15 oz) Mexican-style chili beans with liquid

Instructions:

- In Dutch oven, brown ground beef.
- Drain well.

- Add onions and cook until tender. Add other ingredients and cook (uncovered) for about 45 minutes.
- Ladle into serving bowls and top with cheese and tortilla chips.
- Easy dish for a large group of people.

Cheesy Spinach Lasagna

Ingredients

Sauce

- 4 yellow onions, chopped
- 2 tablespoons sugar
- 4 tablespoons olive oil
- ¼ teaspoon salt
- 16 cloves garlic, minced
- ¼ teaspoon pepper
- 4, 28 ounce cans whole tomatoes
- 2.5 tablespoons oregano
- 1 teaspoon crushed red pepper
- 8 tablespoons tomato paste
- Salt and pepper to taste

Filling

- 64 ounces ricotta cheese
- 1 cup parmesan cheese
- 2 cups fresh basil
- ½ teaspoon black pepper
- 4 eggs
- 3 pounds spinach, steamed

Lasagna
- 18 strips lasagna noodles, uncooked
- 32 ounces mozzarella, shredded
- 3 pounds spinach, steamed and drained well

Instructions:
- Heat oil in a large pot. Add onion, salt, pepper, and olive oil. Add garlic, red pepper, and tomato paste. Stir until combined.
- Add tomatoes and oregano. Cook 20 minutes. Add salt and pepper to taste. Remove from heat.
- While the sauce simmers, add half of the filling ingredients into a food processor. Pulse until combined. Repeat with remaining ingredients. Cover and refrigerate until ready to assemble lasagna.
- Spray the pan with oil. Spread 4 cups of the sauce in the bottom of the pan. Lay 6 uncooked lasagna noodles on top.
- Spread 3 cups of the filling over the noodles. Top with 2 cups of spinach and 8 ounces of cheese. Repeat twice. Add 16 ounces of cheese to the last layer.
- Bake and serve.

Graduated Grilled Cheese

Ingredients
- 4 slices sourdough bread
- ½ cup button mushroom, sliced
- 1 medium yellow onion, sliced
- ¼ teaspoon black pepper

- ¼ teaspoon dried basil
- 2 slices swiss cheese
- 4 slices tomato, thinly sliced
- ¼ teaspoon garlic powder
- ¼ teaspoon onion powder
- Dash of cayenne pepper
- 2 slices sharp cheddar cheese
- 2 tablespoons unsalted butter, softened

Instructions:

- Preheat a University of Tennessee Skillet over medium heat, 4-5 minutes. Add sliced onion, mushrooms, 1 tablespoon butter, and seasonings. Sauté until vegetables are tender, 5-7 minutes.
- While onions and mushrooms are sautéing, butter one side of each piece of bread. Remove sautéed onion and mushrooms from the skillet.
- Assemble the grilled cheese. Place one slice of bread, butter side down, on the skillet. Place one piece of Swiss cheese and half of the sauté mixture on the bread. Add two slices of tomato, one slice of cheddar cheese, and another slice of bread, butter side up. Press sandwich with spatula. Cook until bread is golden brown and cheese is melted, 3-4 minutes per side.
- Repeat with remaining grilled cheese ingredients. Slice diagonally and serve immediately.

Classic Pizza Dough

Ingredients

- 3 cups bread flour, divided
- 1 teaspoon salt
- 1 packet (¼ ounces) active dry rapid-rise yeast
- 1 ½ teaspoons honey
- 1 tablespoon olive oil
- 1 ¼ cups lukewarm water

Instructions:

- In a large mixing bowl, mix ½ cup flour with yeast and salt. Dissolve honey in lukewarm water and add to mixture. Add olive oil.
- In the bowl of a mixer, or using a wooden spoon, mix for 3 minutes. Mix in remaining flour (dough should be only slightly sticky.)
- Knead dough on a floured surface until smooth, approximately 5 minutes.
- Place dough in a lightly oiled bowl and cover with plastic wrap. Let rise for 10 minutes in a warm place.
- Punch dough down and divide in half. Allow to rise for 10 additional minutes. Punch down and spread one of the halves by hand or roller onto your Cast Iron Baking Pan.
- Add toppings of your choice and place in a preheated 450 degrees Fahrenheit oven for 8-10 minutes, or until crust is golden brown. Cool 2-3 minutes before cutting or serving.

Campfire Pizza

Ingredients

- Prepared pizza dough

- 2 cups mozzarella, shredded
- ¼ cup pizza sauce
- ½ cup yellow onion, sliced
- ½ cup green bell pepper, sliced
- 6 ounces pepperoni, sliced
- ½ cup mushrooms, sliced
- Oil, for coating griddle.

Instructions:

- Prepare 2 beds of coals. Set the Cook-It-All's domed skillet/wok in one of the beds of coals.
- Preheat to high heat (Tip: you can use this time to sauté veggie toppings, if desired).
- Oil the griddle side of the Cook-It-All. Roll out pizza dough and place on griddle, leaving an inch around the edge for the domed piece to lay.
- Place the griddle with pizza dough over medium coals. Spread sauce around pizza dough.
- Quickly add toppings and cover with cheese.
- Cover with preheated dome. Fill dome with hot coals and cook until cheese has melted and crust begins to brown (5-10 min).

Cast-Iron Apple-Blackberry Crumble With Sour Cream Whip

Ingredients

Crumb Topping
- 3/4 c. all-purpose flour, spooned and leveled
- 3 tbsp. granulated sugar
- 1 tsp. ground cinnamon
- 1/2 c. packed brown sugar
- 8 tbsp. (1 stick) cold unsalted butter, cut into pieces
- 1/4 tsp. ground cardamom
- 1/2 tsp. kosher salt
- 1 c. old-fashioned rolled oats
- 3/4 c. pecans, chopped

Apple-Blackberry Filling
- Unsalted butter, for pan
- 2 c. blackberries
- 4 lb. apples (such as Golden Delicious and Gala), peeled, cored, and cut into 1/2-inch wedges
- 1 tbsp. lemon zest plus 2 tablespoons fresh lemon juice
- 3 tbsp. cornstarch
- 2/3 c. granulated sugar
- 3/4 tsp. kosher salt

Sour Cream Whip
- 1 c. heavy cream
- 1/4 c. confectioners' sugar
- 1 c. sour cream
- 1 tsp. pure vanilla extract

Instructions:
- Whisk together flour, brown sugar, granulated sugar, cinnamon, cardamom, and salt in a bowl. Add butter. Add

oats and pecans and press mixture into small clumps. Freeze while preparing filling.
- Preheat oven. Butter a skillet. Toss together apples, blackberries, sugar, cornstarch, lemon zest and juice, and salt in a bowl. Transfer to prepared skillet. Scatter topping over fruit.
- Bake.

Make Sour Cream Whip:
- Beat together heavy cream, sour cream, confectioners' sugar, and pure vanilla extract with an electric mixer on medium speed until soft peaks form, 1 to 2 minutes.

Skillet S'mores

Ingredients

- 1/3 c. all-purpose flour, spooned and leveled, plus more for working
- 1/3 c. graham or whole-wheat flour, spooned and leveled
- 1 tsp. ground cinnamon
- 1/2 tsp. Kosher salt
- 1/4 tsp. baking soda
- 3 tbsp. unsalted butter, at room temperature
- 1/3 c. packed light brown sugar
- 2 tsp. Honey
- 1 large egg
- 1/2 tsp. pure vanilla extract

- 1 1/2 c. semisweet chocolate chips
- 6 s'more marshmallows (such as S'moreMallows)

Instructions:

- Preheat oven to 350°F with the racks in the middle and top positions. Line two baking sheets with parchment paper. Whisk together flours, cinnamon, salt, and baking soda in a bowl.
- Beat butter and sugar on medium speed with an electric mixer until light and fluffy, 1 to 2 minutes. Beat in honey until combined. Beat in egg and vanilla until combined. Reduce mixer speed to low and slowly beat in flour mixture
- Scoop dough (about 1 1/2 tablespoons each), 2 inches apart, on prepared baking sheets. Bake, one sheet at a time on the middle rack, until golden brown around edges, 9 to 10 minutes. Cool on baking sheets on wire racks for 5 minutes; remove to the racks to cool completely
- Place 12 (3.5-inch) cast-iron skillets or 1 (9-inch) cast-iron skillet on a rimmed baking sheet. Fill with chocolate chips, dividing evenly. Top with cookies
- Use a serrated knife to cut marshmallows in half crosswise; use a 2-inch star-shaped cookie cutter to cut into shapes (discard excess marshmallow). Top cookies with marshmallow stars
- Bake, on the top rack, until chocolate is melted, 4 to 5 minutes. Switch oven to broil. Broil until marshmallows are golden brown, about 30 seconds. Serve immediately.

Skillet Mac And Cheese With Sausage And Bell Peppers

Ingredients

- 1 lb pork sausage
- 2 bell peppers , diced
- 8 oz elbow macaroni , dry
- 18 oz marinara sauce
- 18 oz water
- 1/3 cup half and half
- 1/3 cup mozzarella cheese

Instructions

- In a large skillet cook sausage on medium heat, until meat is brown. Drain off fat.
- Add diced bell peppers, dried elbow macaroni, marinara sauce, and water. Bring to boil; reduce heat to simmer. Simmer, covered, for about 20 minutes until macaroni is tender, occasionally stirring.
- Add half and half, sprinkle with cheese, and mix everything well. Remove from heat, cover and let it sit for about 2 minutes or until cheese melts.

Creole Rice Skillet With Andouille Sausage

Ingredients

- 1-2 tablespoons grass-fed butter or lard
- 1 onion, chopped
- 1 bell pepper, chopped
- 2 cups cooked rice, any variety

- 4 andouille sausage links, cooked and chopped
- 1½ cups or 1 drained and rinsed can of red kidney beans
- 1 teaspoon salt
- 1 teaspoon black pepper
- 1 teaspoon onion powder
- 2 teaspoons garlic powder
- 1 tablespoon paprika (I use smoked paprika but any kind will do)
- ¼ teaspoon red pepper flakes or cayenne pepper (or both)
- 1 teaspoon oregano
- 1 teaspoon thyme

Instructions

- In a cast iron skillet, heat the butter or lard over medium heat. Saute the onion and bell pepper until they begin to soften.
- Add the rice, sausage and red beans. Stir and let cook until warmed through.
- Add the spices and stir until completely coated. Serve warm in the skillet.

Skillet Green Beans

Ingredients

- 1 lb. green beans
- 1 tbsp. soy sauce
- 1 1/2 tsp. sesame oil

Instructions:

- Preheat oven to 400 degrees F. Meanwhile, in a large cast-iron skillet, toss green beans with soy sauce and sesame oil. Roast, tossing midway through, until just crispy, 15 to 20 minutes.

Potato Cake With Tart Apples And Jarlsberg

Ingredients

- 1/4 c. olive oil
- 8 medium potatoes
- 2 medium Granny Smith apples
- 1 medium onion
- 1/2 c. chopped fresh parsley
- 1 1/4 tsp. salt
- 1/2 tsp. Freshly ground pepper
- 1/2 c. finely grated Jarlsberg
- butter

Instructions:

- Preheat oven to 425 degrees F. Coat inside of a 12-inch cast-iron skillet with olive oil; set aside.
- In a large bowl, toss together potatoes, apples, onion, parsley, salt, and pepper. Spread half the potato mixture in skillet, scatter with cheese, then top with remaining potato mixture. Cover with a piece of lightly buttered foil and bake for 40 minutes.

- Remove foil and continue to bake until potatoes are tender and top is lightly browned, about 20 more minutes. Increase oven to broil and cook until top begins to crisp, about 2 minutes. Sprinkle with parsley. Cool slightly before serving.

Savory Dutch Baby

Ingredients

- ¾ cup whole milk, room temperature
- 3 large eggs, room temperature
- 3 tablespoons unsalted butter, melted, slightly cooled, divided
- ½ cup all-purpose flour
- 2 tablespoons cornstarch
- ½ teaspoon kosher salt
- ½ teaspoon freshly ground black pepper

Instructions:

- Place a medium ovenproof skillet, preferably cast iron, in center of oven and preheat oven to 450°. Let skillet heat at least 25 minutes total (prepare your toppings while you wait).
- Blend eggs in a blender on high speed until very frothy, about 1 minute. With motor running, gradually stream in milk, then 2 Tbsp. butter; blend another 30 seconds. Add flour, cornstarch, salt, and pepper and blend just to combine. (This batter doubles well if you want to scale up.)

- Carefully remove skillet from oven and swirl remaining 1 Tbsp. butter in skillet to coat. Immediately pour batter into skillet (butter will brown quickly, so have batter at the ready to prevent burning). Bake pancake until puffed and brown around edges, 20–25 minutes. It will begin to deflate as soon as it comes out. Top as desired.

Skillet Phyllo Pie With Butternut Squash, Kale, And Goat Cheese

Ingredients

- 3 tablespoons olive oil, plus more for brushing
- 2 medium red onions, finely chopped
- ½ small butternut squash (about 1 pound), peeled, cut into ¾-inch pieces
- 1½ teaspoons chopped thyme
- ½ teaspoon crushed red pepper flakes
- 1 bunch Tuscan kale, ribs and stems removed, thinly sliced crosswise
- 2 large eggs, beaten to blend
- 3 ounces Parmesan, grated
- 1 teaspoon finely grated lemon zest
- Kosher salt, freshly ground pepper
- 8 ounces frozen phyllo pastry, thawed (half a 1-pound package)
- 4 ounces fresh goat cheese or feta, crumbled

Instructions:

- Place a rack in lower third of oven; preheat to 400°. Heat 3 Tbsp. oil in a large ovenproof skillet over medium. Add onions and cook, stirring occasionally, until softened but not browned, 6–8 minutes. Add squash and cook, stirring occasionally, until almost tender, 8–10 minutes. Mix in thyme and red pepper flakes and transfer to a medium bowl; let cool. Wipe out and reserve skillet.

- Add kale, eggs, Parmesan, and lemon zest to squash mixture and gently mix to combine; season with salt and pepper. Layer phyllo sheets inside reserved skillet. Spoon kale-and-squash mixture into phyllo and dot top with goat cheese. Brush edges of phyllo lightly with oil and fold over filling, overlapping slightly, leaving center exposed.

- Cook pie over medium heat until bottom of pastry is just golden (carefully lift up on one side with a heatproof rubber spatula so that you can take a peek), about 3 minutes. Transfer skillet to oven and bake pie until kale is wilted and tender and phyllo is golden brown and crisp, 20–25 minutes. Let pie cool in skillet at least 15 minutes before slicing into wedges.

One-Skillet Chicken With Buttery Orzo

Ingredients

- Kosher salt, freshly ground pepper
- 6 skin-on, bone-in chicken thighs (about 2 pounds total), patted dry
- 3 tablespoons unsalted butter, divided
- 1 fennel bulb, chopped, plus fronds, chopped
- 1 leek, white and pale green parts only, chopped
- 8 ounces orzo

- ⅓ cup dry white wine
- 2½ cups low-sodium chicken broth, divided
- 1 tablespoon fresh lemon juice
- 1 teaspoon finely grated lemon zest

Instruction

- Preheat oven to 400°. Rain salt and then some pepper all over chicken. Heat 2 Tbsp. butter in a medium cast-iron skillet over medium-high. Nestle chicken, skin side down, in skillet in a single layer with no gaps (if you can't quite fit them all, wait until chicken shrinks slightly, then puzzle in the remaining pieces). Cook until meat is opaque around the edges and skin is deep golden brown, 6–8 minutes. Turn chicken skin side up and transfer skillet to oven; bake, uncovered, until chicken is cooked through, 10–15 minutes. Transfer chicken to a plate.
- Set same skillet over medium; combine fennel bulb and leek in skillet and sprinkle in some salt and pepper. Cook, tossing occasionally, until leek is looking golden around the edges, about 5 minutes. Add orzo and cook until pasta is darkened (it will take on a brown hue) to a nice nutty brown in spots and toasty smelling, about 3 minutes. Pour in wine and cook, stirring, until liquid is evaporated, about 1 minute. Add broth ½ cup at a time, stirring constantly and letting broth absorb before adding more, until orzo is tender and broth is mostly absorbed but pan is not dry, 10–15 minutes.
- Remove skillet from heat, Taste and add more salt and pepper to your liking; mix in lemon juice and remaining 1 Tbsp. butter, then chopped fennel fronds. Pile chicken on top and finish with lemon zest.

Cast-Iron Pizza With Fennel And Sausage

Ingredients

- 12 oz. store-bought pizza dough, room temperature
- 5 Tbsp. extra-virgin olive oil, divided
- 8 oz. sweet Italian sausage, casings removed
- Kosher salt
- ⅓ cup prepared marinara
- ¾ cup coarsely grated low-moisture mozzarella
- ½ small fennel bulb, very thinly sliced
- 3 garlic cloves, very thinly sliced
- Crushed red pepper flakes and torn basil leaves (for serving)

Instructions:

- Place a rack in top-most position of oven; preheat to 475°. Place dough on a work surface; drizzle with 1 Tbsp. oil, turning to coat. Stretch out to a 10" round and cover loosely with plastic wrap.
- Heat 1 Tbsp. oil in a large cast-iron skillet over medium. Cook sausage, breaking up into small pieces with a wooden spoon, until browned in spots and cooked though, 5–8 minutes. Transfer sausage to a small bowl.
- Remove skillet from heat and carefully lay dough inside (use spoon to help you extend dough all the way to the edges). Season with salt, then spread marinara over entire surface of dough. Top with mozzarella, then fennel, garlic, and cooked sausage. Drizzle with another 2 Tbsp. oil. Peek underneath the crust—the bottom should be golden brown and crisp from residual heat in the skillet. If it's not, set over medium-low and cook until crust is golden brown, about 3 minutes.
- Transfer skillet to oven and bake pizza on top rack until crust is golden brown around the edges and cheese is browned in spots and bubbling all over, 10–14 minutes. Let cool 5 minutes, then top with red pepper flakes and basil. Sprinkle with more salt and drizzle with remaining 1 Tbsp. oil.

Skillet Peach Cobbler

Ingredients

- 2 cups all-purpose flour
- 1 1/2 cups sugar
- 2 teaspoons baking powder
- 2 teaspoons salt
- 2 large eggs, beaten to blend
- 1 1/2 cups crème fraîche, divided
- 1 cup whole milk
- 2 teaspoons vanilla extract
- 1/4 cup (1/2 stick) unsalted butter
- 2 pounds peeled, pitted peaches, each cut into 1/2 inch wedges (about 2 cups)
- 1 cup Lord Grey's Peach Preserves (click for recipe)
- 1 cup chilled heavy cream
- 2 tablespoons sugar

Instructions

- Preheat oven to 350°. Whisk first 4 ingredients in a medium bowl. Whisk eggs, 1/2 cup crème fraîche, milk, and vanilla in a medium bowl. Add egg mixture to dry ingredients; whisk until smooth. Melt butter in a 12 inch cast-iron skillet over medium heat. Swirl pan to coat with butter. Remove from heat.
- Add batter to pan. Scatter fresh peaches over, then spoon dollops of preserves evenly over batter. Bake until a tester inserted into center of cobbler comes out clean, 45-50 minutes. Let cool slightly. Meanwhile, whip cream in a medium bowl to form soft peaks. Fold in sugar and

remaining 1 cup crème fraîche. Cut cobbler into wedges and serve with whipped cream mixture.

www.ingramcontent.com/pod-product-compliance
Lightning Source LLC
Chambersburg PA
CBHW071456070526
44578CB00001B/367